TEA PARTY ON SAFARI

TEA PARTY ON SAFARI

The Hunt for American RINO

GREG FETTIG

iUniverse, Inc.
Bloomington

Tea Party on Safari
The Hunt for American RINO

iUniverse books may be ordered through booksellers or by contacting:

iUniverse
1663 Liberty Drive
Bloomington, IN 47403
www.iuniverse.com
1-800-Authors (1-800-288-4677)

ISBN: 978-1-4759-2570-8 (sc)
ISBN: 978-1-4759-2571-5 (hc)
ISBN: 978-1-4759-2572-2 (e)

Library of Congress Control Number: 2012908423

Printed in the United States of America

iUniverse rev. date: 05/25/2012

CHAPTER 1

The Proverbial Last Straw

"He's going to be a target of the Tea Party in 2012." That simple proclamation to a *Washington Post* reporter on June 22, 2010, propelled me on a journey that I could not have fathomed at the time—a journey fraught with twists and turns as well as triumph and failure and punctuated with bribes, threats, doubt, mistrust, and betrayal. A journey on a road not well traveled, void of sign posts and direction and with no speed limit, enticingly inviting.

Six-term US Senator Richard Lugar of Indiana had announced the day before that he intended to vote for the confirmation of Elena Kagan to the US Supreme Court, which prompted reporter Amanda Erickson to seek comment from me to gauge reaction from Tea Party activists in Indiana. Her inquiry for comment came to me through a tongue-in-cheek e-mail address that I had set up more as comic relief than as a serious political credential. Dismayed by the destruction of our economy by our newly elected president, I set up an e-mail account that expressed my dissatisfaction with the Obama administration. I was surprised that the *Washington Post* even knew of me at this early stage of the Tea Party movement, let alone was able to track me down through a seldom-used satirical e-mail account.

Senator Lugar's vow, to the dismay of the Tea Party, came on the heels of an equally opposed vote less than a year earlier for liberal Justice Sonia Sotamayor. Sotamayor is a believer in social justice, liberal justification for righting perceived wrongs in society. This vote to confirm the leftist judge was just one of many votes in Lugar's career, but none was more detrimental to the nation. It was the final straw for the conservative Tea Party and set into motion a backlash the senator and the establishment had never before experienced.

On August 5, 2010, Senator Lugar followed through with his pledge and voted for the confirmation of Elena Kagan to the Supreme Court of the United States. Later that day, Fox News quoted Kosciusko County Silent No More's Monica Boyer of Warsaw, Indiana, as saying that Lugar's vote was the last straw. Her group had flooded Lugar's local offices with hundreds of phone calls voicing opposition to his planned vote. Now they pledged to turn their anger into action. That evening they called an emergency meeting to discuss ideas on how to defeat Lugar at the conclusion of his sixth term in 2012. Several angry Hoosiers attended a meeting that served as a therapeutic airing of complaints and frustrations but did not produce a realistic means of defeating a stubborn and condescending senator. Nevertheless, something was happening in Indiana that had not been witnessed before, and the rumblings were beginning to be felt. A seismic shift was occurring, and it would rock the establishment with fear.

My involvement in the Tea Party at this point included cofounding and serving as president of Hoosier Patriots. Later I would cofound America ReFocused. My strategy in the movement was to take my fight to the belly of the beast, the place where nearly all of America's problems were created, which led me to Washington, DC, nearly a dozen times. Some of my accomplishments included asking for and receiving three seats on the Indiana Republican Party's Platform Committee, speaking at their convention, and later speaking at the FreedomWorks-sponsored September 12, 2010, march on Washington.

My reasoning for going to the nation's capital was to cultivate relationships with like-minded conservative groups and individuals with the goal of using their help in our efforts at home. There was not a how-to manual for the Tea Party, but I have always subscribed to the belief that the quickest way to any given point is a straight line. Time was too short to play by the establishment's rules, and besides, I had an incredible disdain for the establishment. Once a staunch Republican, I took offense at both political parties for being culpable in the economic crisis facing the nation. I was now making up my own rules as I went along, and it felt good; no party would own me. The stifling regulations and policies that the Obama administration was imposing on the nation found a population retreating and cowering in the fear of uncertainty. The Tea Party embodied the freedom-loving spirit and can-do attitude that once made America great, and it was from the Tea Party that America would be saved. This was where I would be calling home from now on.

The newfound friends and allies that I cultivated during my many trips to Washington included sympathetic politicians, media contacts, and national conservative organizations. Among these were FreedomWorks, Club for Growth, Americans for Tax Reform, Americans for Prosperity, Fox News, the *Wall Street Journal*, CNN, the BBC, Reuters, the *New York Times*, and dozens of Tea Party group leaders from around the nation and even overseas in Australia, Italy, and Israel.

On November 3, 2010, I answered my ringing phone to the question, "What do you think about taking out Senator Lugar?" My response was, "You do mean *vote* him out, right?" I had heard of Monica Boyer and her efforts in northeastern Indiana, but until this day, our paths had not crossed. That was soon to change.

Indiana's nearly eighty Tea Party groups are as diverse as the landscape of the state itself. In the 2010 US senatorial election to fill the vacant seat of retiring Senator Evan Bayh, the dozens of groups rallied around four of the five republican candidates in the primary. The one candidate that they all could agree on not backing was the GOP establishment pick. Financed through the National Republican Senatorial Committee, Dan Coats was considered to be a Washington insider whose day in the sun had passed and who was not the solution to today's problems. Coats had served as Indiana's senator before, from 1989 to 1999, but now he was unwelcome and resented for entering our race after being away from the state for over ten years.

The various Tea Party groups from around the Hoosier state had all fallen in love with different candidates and refused to rally around one candidate to face the establishment's pick. Each candidate had his or her own following of supporters (political groupies, as I like to call them) that fell in love with them and would not consider any other, none more so than State Senator Marlin Stutzman from northeastern Indiana, a hotbed of Tea Party activism. This was the first election cycle in which the Tea Party took an active role in political campaigning. In retrospect, we supported two of the three politicians in the race and barely noticed the two political novices, whom we as the Tea Party should have embraced for being from the common citizenry. One of these two fared so poorly that he will not likely ever run as a candidate again. The experience left him bitter and disheartened to the point that he has left the Tea Party completely. Not surprisingly, Dan Coats won the May primary with just 39 percent of the vote and went on to win the Senate seat in the November election. Although Coats has performed fairly well to date, the Tea Party was beaten not only by the National Republican Senatorial Committee and their chosen candidate but by itself. The Tea Party group's performance was ridiculed and mocked, and some proclaimed the Tea Party dead in Indiana. The *Daily Beast* issued on May 5, one day after the primary, a stinging criticism of our miserable failure. They stated that the Tea Party in Indiana was irrelevant, a band of amateur political activists determined to go it alone in the stubborn belief that the strength of the Tea Party was derived from each of the several dozens of groups working independently of one another, falsely assuming that we would all somehow arrive at a common destination as if by magic. Six months later, the Indiana Tea Party groups were given a rare opportunity to test whether they had learned their lesson. The credibility of the movement and its very existence were at stake and with it the fate of the nation.

"Let's do it," I said to Boyer, and with that, one of the most organized grassroots efforts anywhere in the nation took form and set its sights on the Republican establishment's most senior icon. A thirty-plus year RINO, or Republican in Name Only, was about to become the next victim of the restless Tea Party. It would prove to be a wild ride.

CHAPTER 2

Anybody Up for a Safari?

Boyer and her board at Kosciusko County Silent No More agreed to meet with me in Fishers, Indiana, for our first formal meeting as Hoosiers for a Conservative Senate. Monica would be accompanied by three of her board members as well as an Elkhart County Tea Party activist whom she had recruited for the cause. I would be joining them in our meeting along with a Bartholomew County Tea Party activist whom I had met in, of all places, Washington, DC.

Our first meeting took place at the Frederick-Talbott Inn, a bed-and-breakfast establishment that had offered their conference center to us as a contribution to the movement. I had first met the owner of the inn and her husband at a Tea Party rally I had spoken at earlier in the year. She approached me afterward and told me of the struggles her inn was having as a result of the economic disaster the country was suffering. She wanted to fight back, and she graciously offered her facility should I ever have a need for a meeting place. It would soon play a historical role in the retirement plans we were making for our wayward senator.

My participation in Hoosiers for a Conservative Senate was contingent on two conditions. The first was that in order to have any chance of defeating a well-entrenched, establishment politician, we had to nationalize our senate race. We also had to identify and isolate any groups that would try to thwart our efforts, and this included fellow Tea Party groups if necessary. Enlisting the media in this endeavor would be critical to our success, but doing so was met with far more resistance from some on our board and from the various Tea Party groups around the state than I initially anticipated.

It was my position that the first group out of the gate to make the case for defeating Senator Lugar would be seen as the preeminent group. To achieve this title, we had to work with the press to get the word out about our existence. To move forward effectively and be worthy of such a title would require nothing less than a Herculean effort and a large dose of Providence. We were confident that we would have the latter. Our faith in God and belief that His hand was in our movement sustained our confidence during very trying times. Many, many prayers were made for the necessary tools and resources to be made available for the successful completion of our mission. Those resources, more often than not, were provided when we most needed them.

We invited a Fox News reporter to our first meeting and offered him an exclusive story if he would document our efforts and release our story at a time we determined to be most beneficial to our cause. The reporter agreed but was a no-show on the day of our first meeting. This proved to be a blessing, as it freed us to be able to use any and all media that we could muster. The media would be essential in nationalizing our race and enlisting the help of all who shared our principles and goals. The race had to be nationalized for there to be any possibility of bringing down an establishment RINO who undoubtedly would have the financial support of donors in Washington, New York, and all points in between. Some in our committee were relieved that the Fox reporter did not come, but the media involvement issue was far from dead. The dissension was caused by two basic concerns: distrust of the press and the belief that the committee was merely seeking publicity for itself. A big-picture mentality was in order, and it was going to have to be painted for all to see.

The first order of business for the Hoosiers for a Conservative Senate committee was to establish a mission statement that would leave no doubt as to what our objective was and would plant seeds of doubt in the minds of past Lugar supporters that he no longer represented Hoosiers' best interests. I was not afraid to use every tactical advantage that we could, and knew that our mission statement could very well get people to realize that Lugar was not conservative after all. This statement had to espouse the beliefs of our movement. It had to be much like the documents of our founding fathers: easy to understand and righteous. Here is what we came up with: "To ensure the United States senatorial representation of Indiana reflects conservative values and is in strict adherence with the Constitution of the United States as worded and originally intended by the writers of this sacred document."

As the committee read aloud this simple, descriptive proclamation, the very fabric of our core values, our sole reason for existence, we stood resolute in the knowledge that our mission was indeed a noble and righteous one. Senator Lugar could not pass the litmus test that our statement required. His votes for Justices Sotamayor and Kagan, both of whom proclaimed under oath that they would look to social justice and international law in reaching their decisions, were more than enough to disqualify him from consideration. His support for blanket amnesty for illegal aliens and his votes for the auto and Wall Street bailouts left no question that our senator had failed miserably to meet any criteria for being conservative.

The remainder of that first meeting was spent discussing how we were going to win the support and enlist the help of the many Tea Party groups around the state. Up to this point, there had not been a comprehensive demographic study of the movement in the state. Each of us knew of a few group leaders in our own areas, but none of us could say that we knew all the Tea Party groups or even how many groups existed in Indiana. Compiling the data that we mined in our efforts to fully understand our movement within our state's borders proved to be eye-opening. There were at least eighty Tea Party groups from one end of the state to the other, ranging from small groups of ten to twenty people to powerful groups of over five hundred. The combined membership of all these groups gave us a potential army of over twenty-five thousand political activists. Assuming that each of these people had the ability to influence on average ten more people who were not already included in our data, we had the potential to have two hundred fifty thousand people to take into battle against the establishment. We did not know all these people, but all we had to do was get to know the leaders of the eighty Tea Party groups and let them carry the message on down the line. There were three group leaders that every Tea Party in the state knew of, and our opinion of the three was less than favorable. These three were a cancer on the movement, and I referred to them as the toxic trio. When possible, we avoided them outright; otherwise they had to be appeased or coerced. Although I personally had experience with only one of them, I knew their reputations, and my second condition for participation in Hoosiers for a Conservative Senate was that these three groups would either have to be included somehow or isolated and cast into irrelevancy for the good of the cause. I knew this was tantamount to a declaration of war within our own family, but one does not allow a family member to embarrass and undermine the welfare of the family as a whole. As the fifth of nine children, I was well suited for the role of peacemaker—or, if necessary, warrior. It would not be long before I knew which I would be, and that choice would not be of my making.

The next day in the political section of the *Indianapolis Star*'s Sunday edition was a report of a Tea Party event held in downtown Indianapolis the previous day attended by two hundred activists promoting the repeal of President Obama's health-care law. A few people interviewed for that story mentioned their intention to work to defeat Senator Lugar in the 2012 election. Up until this point, these were the people from whom the press sought opinions when it came to Lugar. There also appeared a two-sentence mention of a small gathering that same day in Fishers to plot the political demise of Senator Lugar. Monica and I had issued a press release just days before our meeting announcing the founding of Hoosiers for a Conservative Senate and what we were planning. This simple action was crucial to our success, and we prayed that it would be reported on. We were unquestionably the first out of the gate, and as such, we were the preeminent organization whose mission was to defeat Senator Lugar.

The team had been assembled, the prey identified, and the Tea Party was about to go on safari.

CHAPTER 3

The Hunted Meets the Hunter

The three core principles of the Tea Party are limited government, fiscal conservatism, and free-market capitalism. Every Tea Party group in the nation subscribes to these core beliefs. It is the common DNA shared by all those within the Tea Party family. But as in all of mankind, as our family grew in number and spread over a wider geographic area, our diversity increased.

The Midwest (and Indiana, in particular) is home to a large devoutly religious population. As such, there was no escaping the fact that social and religious issues would be woven into the genetic makeup of the movement's core set of principles.

In October 2010, Congressman Mike Pence of Indiana's sixth district was barnstorming the state in a bus in support of fellow Republican congressional candidates running in the November election. This election proved to be a historical shift of power in the US House of Representatives as well as in nearly every elected position throughout Indiana. Monica attended one of the events on Pence's bus tour and by chance was seated directly behind the congressman. When the opportunity to speak with the congressman presented itself, Monica told Pence of an idea she had been developing.

Monica is an ardent Pence supporter, believes him to be a religiously principled man, and has exquisite faith in him. As such, she felt compelled to share her plans on working to defeat Senator Lugar and sought his advice.

Pence quoted scripture saying essentially that when one finds oneself at odds with another, one righteously should seek reconciliation with that individual if possible before seeking confrontation. He went on to offer a meeting with the senator to facilitate that possible reconciliation. Monica was quick to tell me of this encounter at the very start of our partnership and also told me that she was committed to following through with a meeting should it be arranged.

I have been called a cynic on more than one occasion in my life, and that characteristic was on full display in my judgment of the Pence offer. My political instincts told me that Congressman Pence, a party establishment loyalist, did not want to see the boat rocked. At the very least, Pence would not publicly support a challenge against Lugar. It was speculated at the time that Pence would either be a candidate in Indiana's gubernatorial race in 2012 or seek the presidency. He could not, as a Tea Party favorite, risk having his loyalties between the grassroots movement and the GOP establishment tested. If they were, Pence would be forced to choose the GOP. I believe that is why he offered to arrange a meeting with Lugar. Reconciliation would calm the restless Tea Party and provide a smooth road for Pence's political career.

Monica was convinced that Pence would follow through with his promise and arrange a meeting. She told me that I should expect and be ready for it. Almost the entire month of November 2010 passed, and we still had not heard from Pence or Lugar. Monica suggested that perhaps Congressman Pence had forgotten his pledge and that we should seek the meeting on our own in the spirit in which Pence had recommended it.

Monica sent an e-mail to Senator Lugar's offices, and we waited. Then in early December we received notice from Lugar's staff that the senator would indeed like to meet with the two of us. To this day, we do not know if the meeting came to pass due to efforts of Congressman Pence or if Lugar himself was rattled by the thought that for the first time in his career, fellow Republicans were plotting his defeat.

As much as he tried to distance himself from the Senate race and not rattle the tea cup, Congressman Pence was inextricably linked to this battle. His own political aspirations, party allegiances, divided loyalties, and the test of principles from the Tea Party were on a collision course.

The Lugar camp offered us an opportunity to meet with the senator at 8:00 a.m. on Monday, December 13, 2010. We had less than two weeks to prepare for this meeting and even less time to accept the offer. There was much discussion and concern about whether it was even wise to meet with the senator. What was there to gain from such a meeting? The senator was a powerful man who had many people and organizations that had a vested interest in keeping him in office. Were we setting ourselves up to be marked should we be audacious enough to confront our esteemed senator? Some within our own ranks went even further, suggesting that Lugar's ties with globalists and other foreign interests would spell calamity for us. It did cast doubt in our minds on whether this meeting was in our best interest, biblical reference or not. Once again, many prayers were cast upward and God's protection humbly requested.

The weekend preceding our meeting with the senator found me in Massachusetts attending the Boston Tea Party. A winter storm was bearing down on the eastern half of the country on Sunday, December 12, the day of my scheduled departure for Indianapolis. The first leg of my journey home took me to Reagan National in Washington, DC. It was after 9:00 p.m. Sunday night, and I had less than twelve hours before the meeting with Lugar. The storm was not going to be outrun, and my flight was delayed in DC. Finally, at 1:00 a.m. on Monday, December 13, I was airborne and headed to Indianapolis. I arrived at 2:30 a.m. and was at last in bed at 3:30 a.m., four and a half hours before the big meeting. Monica had been texting me for hours, worried over the prospect of having to meet the senator alone.

By six o'clock the same morning, I was headed downtown to meet Monica and the senator at the Indianapolis Marriott Hotel. The day was bitterly cold and snowy, and I was operating on less than two hours sleep. Monica and I had agreed to meet at 7:30 a.m. and spend thirty minutes going over our game plan. We had no more than greeted one another when we were approached by two individuals. They were two Lugar staffers, and it was immediately apparent to me that their recognition of us proved that they had done their intelligence work.

We were told that Senator Lugar was in his room reading his paper and ready for the meeting if we did not mind getting started early. It struck me as odd that the former mayor of Indianapolis was in a room at the Marriott Hotel. Why was he in his room and not coming from his house? We would find out later that the senator and his wife had been using a previous address for the past thirty-five years on their voter registration and did not own a home in Indiana. We had stepped into a world that felt foreign, wrong, and threatening.

Senator Lugar greeted us with his trademark warm and smiling demeanor. He could very well have been mistaken for a grandfather meeting with his grandchildren and children for breakfast. We were directed to the buffet, and I noticed that the hotel staff was very much aware that this man was Senator Lugar. After a few pleasantries, we were asked to enjoy our meal, and the senator proceeded to tell us his life story. He beamed with pride as he recounted the family struggles on the farm and how the Lugar family had pulled itself up by its own bootstraps. It occurred to me at that precise moment that I was witnessing a political television advertisement that he would use in his reelection campaign. How could anyone be against a grandfatherly figure who struggled in life to realize the American dream? What would not be part of such a commercial, however, was the fact that due to the senator's own record, the American dream was out of reach for nearly every American, and the nation itself was in jeopardy. I was not buying what he was selling.

Lugar spoke for nearly an hour, his breakfast untouched, before finally he acknowledged that we might have questions of him. Monica began by respectfully thanking him for meeting with us and proceeded to ask why he had voted for Obama's Supreme Court nominees. Over the next hour, we quizzed him on his support of the DREAM Act, the START Treaty, earmarks, and the Federal Reserve. One by one, the senator answered our queries and assured us that his support of all these issues proved that he was indeed a conservative and said he hoped that he could have our support.

The two-and-a-half-hour meeting concluded with his stating to Monica that he was a Methodist, and he then leaned over to me and whispered, "How is your business doing?"

The senator, who tried for over two hours to convince us that he was a kind, gentle, and likeable conservative, not only failed to do so in his answers, but his last comments came across as threats. His mentioning to Monica that he was a Methodist was designed to appeal to her staunch religious beliefs. His question about my business, which I had not mentioned during our meeting, was nothing more than a way of letting me know that they were checking us out. The senator had shown himself willing to use the Chicago-style thug politics of President Obama and Rahm Emanuel, and I could not wait to get home and take a shower to rid myself of the filth of his contempt for us. This certainly did not have a biblical feel to me.

I later told Monica that we would wait to see what the Lugar camp did with this meeting, as I was sure they would try to spin it to their advantage in the media. I wanted them to act first so that we could challenge the falsehoods that I expected to see from them. Much to my surprise, three weeks passed, and the Lugar camp did not make the meeting public. My assessment of this was that Lugar had made a tactical error by meeting with two Tea Party activists and did not want the story made public. Who would have thought that a six-term senator, the highest-ranking Republican in the Senate, would reduce himself to meeting with two unknown and unimportant citizens when he rarely ever met with anyone other than campaign donors? The fact that he had done so proved he was vulnerable, and we had to seize the moment. I decided that a well-placed e-mail might be the spark needed to get the fire going.

On January 5, 2011, Providence once again rang in the form of a phone call from Peter Hamby of CNN. I had met and been interviewed by Hamby in Washington the previous February, and he had reported fairly and accurately on my comments. Peter asked me what I was up to and whether there was anything new to report from Indiana. I was surprised that my e-mail had produced such an immediate response, and I knew that I had to convince him that our meeting with Lugar was newsworthy. I went over the two-and-a-half-hour meeting with Lugar in complete detail, and Hamby was enthralled with the thought of breaking this story. That afternoon, CNN's political ticker ran the headline, "Tea Party Leaders Not Swayed by Lugar Meeting." Our meeting was spelled out in full detail as a national story, and it was capped off by my quote, "We equated it to going out on a football field, shaking hands and flipping the coins, and game on. He wants to win, and we want to win."

CHAPTER 4

---·---

Game Preserve: The Bribe

By the time that the CNN article appeared, Hoosiers for a Conservative Senate had established our core committee, written our mission statement, established ourselves as the preeminent group trying to defeat Senator Lugar, and developed a blueprint of our plan. And we had met with the senator to see if he would surrender.

It seemed that the only thing left to do at this point was to see if anyone was up for a hunt. The result was the largest gathering of Tea Party leaders from around the state ever to be held in Indiana. We sent out e-mails and made phone calls to every Tea Party group that we were aware of. All told, we contacted and invited more than eighty groups, and seventy agreed to attend our meeting. These eighty groups and their members consisted of over twenty-five thousand activists motivated to save their country. That goal would be achieved in part with the removal of Senator Lugar from power.

The purpose of the meeting was to pitch our idea of defeating Lugar by getting the fiercely independent and distrusting groups to agree to unify in a coordinated, cooperative effort. This endeavor would only work if we had a single, universally shared goal. There was not one legitimate Tea Party group anywhere in the state that supported Lugar in the 2012 election, and with that it was clear that our only goal as Hoosiers for a Conservative Senate was to send our senator into retirement by defeating him in Indiana's May 8, 2012, primary. To quell any inkling of distrust or suspicion, we decided not to structure this organization with a few leaders telling the rest of the members what to do. That was not what the Tea Party was about, and we were keenly sensitive to that.

Our meeting was set for January 22, 2011, at Heartland Ministries in Tipton, Indiana. The pastor of Heartland had agreed to offer the use of his church for our historical meeting. I had first met this individual in April 2010 at the Tipton County Courthouse, where he had offered the prayer before a Tax Day rally that I had sponsored. I told the pastor that he was free to say a few words in addition to his prayer, and he did not waste the opportunity to speak his mind. The pastor was at the very least a Tea Party sympathizer in spirit, and I had found yet another ally in our fight. He was in agreement with us that Senator Lugar had to go.

By early January 2011, a little over two months into our journey, everything appeared to be going as planned. We were cautiously optimistic with two weeks to go until our fate would be decided by the collective decision of the seventy Tea Party groups attending our unity meeting. We were confident about how smoothly things were running. Our naiveté, however, was about to come face-to-face with a cold dose of reality. Steven the Snake was about to slither into our world.

On January 13, 2011, eight days after the CNN article, a call came into my office from a man with an Arabic first name and English surname. I recognized the 202 area code immediately—Washington, DC. The caller informed me that his boss was interested in helping the Tea Party and would like to meet with me. I asked him who his employer was, and he said that it was Mr. Steven the Snake. I did not recognize the name and quickly performed a Google search on him. The Snake was worth $3.5 billion and he wanted to fly into Indianapolis and meet with me. Was the Tea Party in Indiana about to become the fortunate recipient of a benevolent donation? I had my suspicions, but it is not every day that a snake worth several billion dollars requests a meeting with you, so I granted his request.

The caller informed me that Mr. Snake would be available to meet with me at noon the following Thursday at the Indianapolis Wyndham Garden Hotel near the airport and would be flying in on his private jet. I agreed to the meeting and then frantically did as much research on this man as I could. I prayed that he was sincere but feared he was a Lugar agent and prepared myself for that possibility. My research on the Snake showed that he was a major contributor to both the Democrats and the Republicans. This is typical behavior for a snake—playing both sides in an attempt to increase the odds of currying favor regardless of outcome.

I also discovered that this fork-tongued serpent had made most of his money in the coal business. That was perplexing, as Lugar had a voting record that had hurt the coal industry and approved of Obama's secretary of energy, Steven Chu, well known for his opposition to coal use. It was hard to tell with certainty where the Snake's allegiance resided, but my gut told me he was an agent of the establishment. In a span of thirty-eight days I had met with a sitting US senator and was about to meet with someone who might be one of the empire's enforcers. Steven the Snake, meet the Tea Party.

At five minutes past noon, January 20, 2011, I was waiting in the bar of the Wyndham Garden Hotel as instructed, and the Snake was late. I proceeded to the front entrance to see if he had had second thoughts and would pull a no-show. Although I had no idea what the Snake looked like, I believed he would not be difficult to spot. It was ten minutes past noon when a black Lincoln Town Car pulled up to the front portico of the hotel and the driver got out and opened the rear driver-side door of the car. Out stepped a man of diminutive stature sporting a black, slicked-back mane and dressed in a black overcoat. I thought for a moment that perhaps the Mafia had arrived, and I hurried back to the bar to appear bored and ready to leave. The Snake approached me with little warmth, although it was the dead of winter, and the creature couldn't be faulted for conforming to its cold-blooded nature. He suggested that we move to the back of the bar, away from the few guests having lunch. I guess it was too much to expect that the Billionaire Snake would buy my lunch. He offered me a Coke instead—one Coke and one Coke only. There were no free refills at the bar.

With no pleasantries exchanged, a two-and-a-half-hour meeting ensued; all meetings with establishment figures seem to be two-and-a-half hours long for some reason—they must have a code or something.

The billionaire started the meeting off by addressing the issues Monica and I had emphasized to Lugar the month before. The details of his questions almost made it seem that he had attended that meeting, but in fact he had not. I may be slow, but I am not that slow; this was a Lugar guy. The Snake said, "Greg, what's the big deal with the START Treaty? You know what? The Russians cheat, but so do we." He was trying to convince me that this was a nonissue and that the treaty was meritless and no cause for worry regarding our national security. Never mind the fact that the Russians have ten thousand more tactical nuclear weapons than we do. The Snake was just getting warmed up.

"Greg, your concern over the DREAM Act and Senator Lugar's support of it is just silly. Do you realize how many millions of unfilled jobs there are in this country?" *Pinch me*, I thought. We were in the middle of the Obama depression, and the only economic boom I had witnessed was in Washington, DC. I was not sure what world Mr. Billionaire Snake was living in, but it sure was not the reality that faced Indiana. In addition, the Tea Party is made up of antiglobalists, and we do not believe in open borders and blanket amnesty for illegal immigrants. Strike two.

Next up for discussion were the Supreme Court nominees. "Yeah, Greg, we kind of scratched our heads on that one too, but who agrees with anyone all the time? Senator Lugar is very conservative, and we must take back the Senate." Strike three.

I had barely gotten a word in and felt it was my turn at bat. The Snake apparently did not play by the rules, and he was intent on winning this game. He then went on to ask what would happen if our candidate did somehow manage to defeat Lugar. No candidate had stepped forward to challenge Lugar yet, although speculation swirled over two likely possibilities. That would open the seat to a Democrat, he reasoned, and he went on to say that we must win the Senate in 2012 in order to stop the Obama agenda. "I know Richard Mourdock," he said. State Treasurer Richard Mourdock is a Tea Party favorite and was thought to be readying a Senate run. "He's a nice guy, but he will not win the general election if he should defeat Senator Lugar in the primary. This Delph guy I haven't met, but there is no way he could win the general election," the Snake explained. State Senator Mike Delph was mentioned regularly as a potential Lugar challenger.

He then asked if I knew how difficult it was to raise campaign funds, particularly in this economic environment. "So if you guys go after Senator Lugar, we are going to have to spend ten million dollars to defend that seat when that money could have been used in Mike Pence's gubernatorial run," the Snake informed me. Mike Pence was running for governor? Who knew, but then again, Mr. Pence had wanted us to play nice with Senator Lugar. I don't like puzzles much, but the pieces to this one were seemingly starting to come together.

Just a few weeks earlier, Lt. Governor Becky Skillman had announced that she would not be seeking the governorship in 2012 due to minor health issues. I was skeptical of that claim at the time, believing that she had been asked to get out of the way for another candidate. Now I was sure she had been pushed aside. The national buzz at this point was that Pence was considering a presidential run, but all the obstacles for a gubernatorial run were being cleared, and I was the next hurdle to be eliminated.

This game that we were playing took on the feel of a high-stakes poker game. I sat emotionless and tried to appear removed from interest. I did not know where this game was headed, but the Snake had plenty of chips left to continue. The stakes were about to get dramatically higher.

The billionaire decided to try to lure me in with a pair of deuces. "Greg, you know, you and a few of your Tea Party friends are obviously politically astute. You might do well to consider attending this fund-raiser that I have every June. It is not your average fund raiser; this one is huge." The Snake played host every summer to a national who's who list of GOP elites at his palatial estate. He said that he would be happy to invite me to this little party of his and that I would have an unprecedented opportunity to network with the likes of Senator Mitch McConnell and others. *Uh, get a clue, Snake. We want to get rid of McConnell as well.* My pair of kings trumped his deuces.

So the game continued as the Snake felt no shame in trying to bribe me with a party invitation. The Snake considered me to be a cheap date and unprincipled and that angered me, but I had to play on to see what he was truly willing to offer. That would tell me how vulnerable Lugar really was. The game wore on for another hour as we tossed political theory at one another. Finally the Snake grew weary of this seemingly endless game and was about to play his ace in the hole.

Again he led with the same appeal. "You could do so much more good in the name of conservatism if you came and played for our side—the Republicans. Do you realize how many open positions on congressmen and senators' staffs there are in Washington?" He did not directly say that Senator Lugar was making the offer, but had I accepted his offer, I would have been working in Washington for a politician. Principled righteousness provides one the protection of a Kevlar vest. *No thank you, Mr. Snake; I will remain in Indiana, working to save my nation, and I work for myself.*

With that, the Snake realized he had run out of chips and abruptly and coldly ended our high-stakes match. I sensed that he was not in the habit of losing. Before he left, he asked me if we were having a party of some sort in the next few days. They knew full well it was to be held in two days on January 22. He gave me his business card and wrote his cell number on the back, asking that I not share it with anyone. "Give me a call next week and let me know how it goes." Yeah, like that was going to happen, but I did share his number with numerous individuals. The following night, Lugar had a country club fund-raiser held in his honor in Carmel, Indiana, and Mr. Snake was on the invitation list as a major Lugar donor.

Only one of us left unscathed by corruption. One man boarded his Town Car to his waiting personal jet; the other climbed into his well-worn pickup truck and headed down the road toward an uncertain future. Another shower, however, was a certainty.

CHAPTER 5

Plotting the Course

Three days before Hoosiers for a Conservative Senate's meeting in Tipton, Indiana, Senator Lugar announced that he would be seeking reelection for an unprecedented seventh term in the US Senate in 2012. Lugar said that this was the earliest he had ever started a reelection bid. We had put him on the defensive. We smelled vulnerability and did not intend to let up on him.

In preparation for our big meeting, some on our committee continued to question why the media should be allowed to observe. Even more frustrating was that many attendees expressed their dissatisfaction with the idea and feared that we would be giving our game plan to Lugar. In the end, the Hoosiers for a Conservative Senate committee did agree to notify the press of the event and invite them to attend. This was a hard-fought battle, and the vote was not unanimous. To win the approval of our committee and the Tea Party groups, we formatted the meeting in two parts. The first was a unity-building mission that we hoped the press would be anxious to report on but would spell our end if unity did not in fact emerge. The second half of our meeting was closed to the press, and that was where we laid out our blueprint for the retirement of Senator Lugar.

I was not going to take no for an answer on the press issue, and I had Monica on my side. This issue consumed many hours of valuable time, and I was frustrated that so many people could not understand why this was an absolute must for the success of our mission, especially after the critically timed CNN article. We issued another press release about the January 22 meeting, and there was a small amount of buzz being generated about it in central Indiana. Even this would not be the last time we had to deal with the press issue.

I once again drew from my national connections and invited FreedomWorks to attend the Tipton event. I also asked the Tea Party in Washington to be ready for a savvy promotional event that we had ready to launch immediately after our meeting. The DC area Tea Party leader immediately agreed to help and went further by offering me the contact information for Tea Party Express. On my drive up to Kokomo for our dress rehearsal the night before the event, I called the spokesperson for Tea Party Express. She said that they had Lugar on their list of possible targets for defeat and agreed to be part of the effort. Our friends were increasing in number and influence, and the Tea Party in Indiana was becoming a formidable force. We would soon see whether the various groups had indeed learned their lesson from the year before. It was nearly showtime, and all eyes would soon be on Indiana.

One of the first things the committee insisted upon was that we would not treat Senator Lugar with any malice or disrespect even though we steadfastly could not support him. The toxic trio had been waging an all-out war of words with Lugar, calling him names like Lex Lugar and proposing campaign slogans like "Dump the Dick" and "Ditch the Dick." We were resolved to run an organization with far more class than that, and with that in mind, our first act would be to request respectfully that the senator step down and retire after the completion of his current term.

During our second meeting as Hoosiers for a Conservative Senate, we came up with the idea of asking our senator to retire. In the course of these discussions, we composed a letter in the form of a scroll that intentionally looked similar to the Declaration of Independence. A board member of Kosciusko County Silent No More was instrumental in producing this scroll, and it proved to be the centerpiece of the unity portion of our statewide meeting. There was even space on the lower third of the scroll for those Tea Party group leaders attending the meeting to sign their names just as our founders did with the Declaration of Independence. The tangible aspect of signing the scroll was designed to have a powerful effect on the attendees, for the symbolism of their signing conveyed agreement in working together for a common cause. This was a beautiful and brilliantly constructed tool for building unity within the Tea Party. However, it had the potential to serve an even greater role for our mission, and that was where the DC area Tea Party and CNN came in.

I suggested that we use this unique document as another media coup for Hoosiers for a Conservative Senate by physically driving the document to Lugar's Washington, DC, offices immediately following the conclusion of our event and personally delivering it to the senator. The DC area Tea Party would greet and join our contingent as a show of national Tea Party unity as they arrived in Washington to deliver the document to Senator Lugar. CNN was informed of our plan and promised to have a film crew waiting outside Lugar's Senate offices. This was going to be fun, and I could not wait to see how much media play we would get from this. We called it the Road Trip to Retirement Tour.

During our outreach to the dozens of Tea Party groups in Indiana, we received numerous expressions of support and offers of help. I had the idea of using them in our unity meeting for strategic purposes. One of our greatest potential adversaries was a member of the toxic trio, and he, oddly enough, had sent us a detailed letter that was long-winded and self-promoting but did include a sentence stating his and his partner's support of our efforts. It was imperative that Hoosiers for a Conservative Senate project these e-mail messages onto the media screens at our meeting for all to see the unity conveyed within them. It also would be our preemptive strike on the toxic trio to expose them as hypocrites should they backpedal from their support.

Before the statewide meeting, the committee of Hoosiers for a Conservative Senate consisted of five people including Monica Boyer and me. It had been decided that we would divide the state by congressional district and that each district would have a representative who would serve on the committee. This format would allow the Tea Party groups to elect four more people to the committee during the unity meeting to establish trust in the committee's legitimacy. As with the other Tea Party groups in the state, in each case the person who had the idea to start the group was the leader of that group. Hoosiers for a Conservative Senate was no different, and as such, five of the nine district representative positions were filled. We had offered one of the district chairs to the ring leader of the toxic trio, Peter the Not Great. Peter was, in his mind, the leader of the Tea Party in Indiana. He told everyone that he practically invented the state movement—sort of like Al Gore invented the Internet—and he had an intense rivalry with Monica. Peter thought on our offer for about a day and decided to decline, but he did send us an e-mail wishing us well; I think he had his fingers crossed when he said that. In his reasoning for declining our offer, he stated that his group was the most credible when it came to vetting candidates in the state and that they were practically best buddies with Richard Mourdock and would be supporting him the moment he announced his candidacy.

The other toxic leader was signed up to attend along with seventy other groups from South Bend to Evansville, Terre Haute to Richmond, Lafayette to Warsaw, New Albany to Rensselaer, and nearly everywhere else. Two leaders from each Tea Party group were allowed to attend as well as three bloggers and all the media we had invited. The committee, cautiously confident and optimistic, concluded the dress rehearsal as we began all our events and meeting—in prayer. One by one, heads bowed and hands linked in a chain as we went around the table and offered prayers to God asking that our unity meeting be blessed with His approval. We had done all that we could do, and the fate of Hoosiers for a Conservative Senate rested in the hands of 140 Tea Party leaders set to flock to Tipton, Indiana, the next morning.

Earlier in the day and thirty miles to the south in Carmel, Indiana, Senator Lugar had issued a press release stating that 420 supporters would be attending a fund-raising dinner hosted in his honor that evening and donating $400,000 to his campaign. This message, laced with arrogance, was directed at us; their hastily planned event was designed to counter what we had planned for the next day. We had once again put the senator on the defensive.

I wondered if the senator knew the story of a ragtag bunch of underfunded patriots humbling King George III.

CHAPTER 6

———— ◆ ————

Peaceful Assembly: The Tea Party Tribes Gather

Twenty-three days before the Indiana Tea Party gathered for safari, a small earthquake rattled Heartland Ministries and the surrounding area. The epicenter was less than ten miles from our gathering site. God had sent a gentle reminder that He was the master of our universe and that we were His servants. If Providence was with us, we would be sending a shockwave of our own from Indiana to Washington, DC, serving notice to all politicians that had ignored or forgotten the Constitution that we the people are their masters and that they are our servants.

The game had been changed, and we were remembering what we had long forgotten as a people. The power resides with the people and not with politicians. When we allowed them, whether through trust, complacency, or apathy, to have more power than was constitutionally legal or just, we willingly surrendered a portion of our freedom. Today we had gathered to reclaim that power. Individually, we would have been ignored. A few of us together would have been mocked. A statewide, coordinated grassroots movement committed to working together, we hoped, would have them quaking in fear that a sleeping populace was coming back from hibernation. We were hungry after a long slumber, and we were ready for a hunt. RINO was what we craved—and a specific one at that.

On January 22, 2010, all roads for the statewide Tea Party movement led to Heartland Ministries just north of the tiny town of Tipton, Indiana. Tipton was where I had received my formal education, and over the last thirty years I had rarely been back other than for an occasional visit. If I ever run out of battles to fight or find the time to do so, I may be inclined to help the Tipton Tea Party clean a house of corruption better known as the Tipton County GOP—a.k.a. Good ol' Boys' Club. But this day my battle was with a much bigger fish in a far larger pond.

The Hoosiers for a Conservative Senate committee nervously waited for the arrival of our guests. In the aftermath of the shooting of Congresswoman Gabrielle Giffords of Arizona, we had decided to hire a Tipton County sheriff's deputy for security precautions. Indianapolis WISH-TV 8 reporter Jim Shella had tried to paint that shooting as the Tea Party's responsibility. He stated in his January 10 blog, "Any talk of Tea Party responsibility in the Arizona shooting of Congresswoman Gabrielle Giffords has apparently had no effect on Tea Party activity here. Greg Fettig of the Indiana Party just sent out a news release confirming plans to hold a January 22 meeting to identify a candidate who might unseat Republican Richard Lugar in the 2012 primary. The release makes no mention of outside events." Shella knew full well that the shooting of Giffords was the work of an unstable man who had Democratic Party sympathies and in no way was a Tea Party member but insinuated that we had responsibility. He also misstated the purpose of our meeting, which was to establish unity, not to select a candidate. This would not be my last run-in with this reporter. Live and learn.

While we were cognizant of the fact that there might be outsiders wishing to disrupt our event, we had not taken into consideration that those within our own ranks could pose a problem. In the excitement of preregistering dozens of guests without knowing everyone in the movement at the time, our check-in procedures left a lot to be desired. We should have had a uniform set of guidelines and strictly enforced rules about what constituted a Tea Party group. We had inadvertently set ourselves up for an interesting day.

More than 140 Tea Party leaders, a gallery of nearly forty Tea Party members, and several members of the media all arrived for our three-hour meeting. Of the seventy-two Tea Party groups that had preregistered to attend, sixty-eight actually showed up. A couple of groups called the morning of our gathering to state that the weather and family illness prevented them from coming. The leader of one group, a supporter of the toxic trio, sent us a late-night e-mail stating that as a 501(c)(4) entity, their board of directors had determined that they could not attend this political event without risking their tax-exempt status. Call me a cynic, but I'm quite certain this bunch never intended to come in the first place. The leaders of this group had been the ones that the press called whenever they wanted comment on Senator Lugar. That was no longer the case, and I believe that as well as their alliance within the toxic trio motivated them not to play nicely with us.

The doors opened to a waiting crowd, many of whom had driven several hours to be a part of this unprecedented meeting. At 10:00 a.m. the crowd included nearly two hundred people, and we were poised to begin. It was time to shine. We had asked Tea Party sympathizer and radio talk show host Pat Miller of WOWO 1190 AM in Fort Wayne to emcee our event. Pat is a dynamic speaker and shared our mission of sending Lugar into a forced retirement. He sprinkled a healthy amount of historical references into his passionate plea for unity. Pat gave a rousing speech about how nearly everyone in the room had supported Senator Lugar at one time or another but over time had become disillusioned with him. With every passing year, we were all becoming more disenchanted with our senator as his record reflected more of the values of the liberal East Coast than those of the crossroads of America. He explained the short history of Hoosiers for a Conservative Senate and how the committee had been chosen. He stressed that all the groups in attendance had started with people taking an initiative. It was critical to the goal of unity that the attendees understand that the Hoosiers for a Conservative Senate committee was credible, that their intentions were pure, and that there were open positions for fair representation. These open positions would be filled that day by attending Tea Party members by a vote of their peers. Miller did a fabulous job of making the crowd receptive to the idea of unity, and then the torch was passed to the Hoosiers for a Conservative Senate committee to continue in that effort.

I started with the analogy of the recent earthquake and the message that our unity would send to the Washington establishment. Then it was time to use the e-mail messages of encouragement and support that we had received and collected during the previous weeks. One by one, the messages were flashed up on the screens, each quote attributed to its author. Quotes had been selected to represent a cross section of the state. Included in these was the message of support from Peter the Not Great and his group. There it was for nearly every Tea Party leader in the state to see. Peter could not now backpedal from his support without exposing himself as the person many of us knew him to be. Somehow, we just knew this was not going to stop him.

The remaining committee members stepped up to the stage and gave their impassioned pleas for unity. Some referenced the frustrations and internal squabbles our founding fathers dealt with, while others addressed the calamity our nation would face if we did not take it back. Now it was time to bring out the big guns—the representatives from FreedomWorks. If any of the Tea Party leaders had concerns about our credibility, they certainly could not doubt the credibility of a powerhouse conservative organization with decades of experience.

FreedomWorks assured the crowd that our mission and organization were far ahead of any they had seen in the nation. They told of Tea Party successes in Utah, where organized efforts had defeated establishment Senator Bob Bennett and replaced him with Tea Party favorite Mike Lee. We were promised support if we bound together in unity and worked in a coordinated fashion. FreedomWorks' confidence in our organization carried weight and commanded respect, and it would prove to be invaluable to our cause.

We had done our best to unify the state Tea Party movement. Now it was up to the 140 leaders to cast their vote of confidence. Our fate would be decided in the next sixty minutes. It was time to introduce the scroll to the audience and read its message encouraging Senator Lugar to retire.

———•———

Honorable Senator Richard G. Lugar,

It is with deep gratitude and respect for your forty-six years of public service to the citizens of Indiana that we approach you with our request. Your distinguished political career began with the Indianapolis Board of School Commissioners and continued with your two terms as Mayor of Indianapolis. Then, in 1976, you began the first of six terms as United States Senator representing the great state of Indiana.

For your decades of dedicated public service and the many accomplishments that have accompanied this admirable career, the people of Indiana are grateful and thank you for your services.

However, with the rise of the conservative consciousness in America, the emergence of the modern-day Tea Party, and your more socially liberal perception of issues, we find ourselves at odds. As representatives of groups from Lake Michigan to the Ohio River, the Wabash Valley to the Whitewater River Valley, and all points in between, we have decided to unite. We are male and female, old and young, rich and poor, with one common goal. We as Hoosiers feel it is our duty to unite behind one candidate who represents our Hoosier values instead of turning a blind eye to national influences and hopelessly voting to slow the progressive takeover of our great nation. Therefore, we have decided to be proactive and reverse the progressive movement by steering Indiana back onto the course our founding fathers envisioned by use of the election process.

So it is with great respect that we convey to you that we cannot and will not support you in the May 2012 primary election and ask you to gracefully consider retirement at the conclusion of your current term.

Very Sincerely,

———•———

The message was roundly approved by the leaders, and they were then asked to come up one by one and put their John Hancock on it. I was cautiously optimistic that this symbol of unity would lead to complete unity in the closed-door second half of our meeting. Nearly 150 signatures adorned our beautifully crafted scroll. It was going to look wonderful hanging in Senator Lugar's Washington office.

The press was then asked to leave so that our closed-door session could begin, but not before many interviews were given and much footage filmed. The press corps in attendance consisted of three bloggers, crews from three TV stations from Indianapolis and Fort Wayne, a team from an Indianapolis talk radio show, several newspaper writers, and a reporter from the Associated Press. We were confident that our story would be told to the state if not the nation.

During the second half of our meeting, we focused on how and why to accomplish our mission. If we did not unify and rally in support of one candidate to challenge Lugar, a multicandidate field would favor Lugar just as it had favored Senator Dan Coats the year before. We still did not have any challengers who had stepped up to confront Lugar, but we knew there would likely be several.

Monica came up with the idea of presenting our plan graphically as a house. Our house would be built on a solid foundation representing our unity and our mission statement. On the main floor of the house resided the need for educating the public about Lugar's liberal voting record. The second floor housed the necessity of educating ourselves about potential candidates through a vetting process. Floor three was occupied by the need for a caucus to vote on the one candidate we would all support, and the final floor held the campaign stage in support of our candidate. Our house was capped with a roof labeled "Conservative Senate," complete with a chimney with a smoke cloud rising from it with the words, "Fueled by the Tea Party, an inexhaustible energy source."

Our last order of business for the day was to organize the dozens of groups into the districts in which they were located. The Hoosiers for a Conservative Senate committee members were from the second, third, fifth, sixth, and ninth districts and served as representatives of those districts. The remaining four districts were open seats for which representatives needed to be nominated and voted on. All nine districts huddled in conversation as well as writing down a list of issues that they wished to discuss. I stepped off the stage and had only begun to mingle with my group in introductions when a voice from the stage broadcasted dissension.

We all turned toward the stage. A young man had taken control of a microphone, inadvertently left live, and the next few moments seemed to pass in slow motion. As I hurried back to the stage, this man said that he believed the Hoosiers for a Conservative Senate board was dictatorial and should step down completely so that all districts could vote in new representatives. After what seemed an eternity, I finally had arrived at the stage, covered the microphone with one hand, and whispered in not so many words that this individual should leave the stage immediately. He backed down and scampered away, but not before causing an incident that I felt had to be addressed immediately. I had no script for this, but the words came out as they needed to. I told the audience that if that was how they all felt, then I personally would step down and let my district vote in a new representative. I asked them to consider, before making their decision, the time invested in this endeavor thus far and the incredible amount of work that was ahead of us. They were also told that this could be a thankless job and that there were going to be attacks from enemies, but if they wanted to dissolve the committee and start completely from scratch, so be it. It was their choice to make.

I was pumped full of adrenaline, perspiring, and angry. Everything we had worked so hard for was at risk. I walked back to where my district members had assembled to applause and an incredible sense of warmth. They were all smiling and clapping and said, "Greg, we unanimously voted for you." The other four Hoosiers for a Conservative Senate committee members retained their positions as well, and we concluded with representatives for every district but the first district.

The young man who had shown more bravado than tact was from district one. He and his friends were not Tea Party members and had falsely represented themselves to gain entry into our meeting. We assumed at the time that they were Lugar operatives sent to disrupt our meeting. The church's pastor spoke with me afterward and told me he had chided the young man, telling him how lucky he was that he was a man of God and that if it were not for that fact he would have taken him out back and paddled him. I loved this man for a reason, and that reason was his righteous defiance of all that was unjust.

The long, emotional roller-coaster ride was over, and we jubilantly celebrated achieving what many naysayers had predicted could not be done. It was done in the house of God, and I felt the shockwave beneath my feet as it rolled, along with our scroll, toward Washington, DC.

CHAPTER 7

Media Envy Sows Seeds of Discontent

The "Road to Retirement Tour" began immediately after our successful unity meeting at Heartland Ministries. Our district nine representative volunteered to serve as courier and drive the scroll to Washington after Monica and I decided we should duck out of the limelight for a while. The media had been a point of contention from the start, and now that publicity for Hoosiers for a Conservative Senate was coming in readily, we thought it wise to lay low for a while. The bribe attempt by Steven the Snake was enough cause for concern, and our gutsy delivery of the scroll was sure to evoke a response. We were trying to deflect some of the arrows being launched our way.

Sunday evening, our courier sent a desperate e-mail to the Hoosiers for a Conservative Senate committee saying that he could not deliver the scroll. When questioned as to why, he responded by saying that it had been defaced and that it could be taken as a threat to the senator. Our courier was spending the night before the delivery in a mountainous area of Virginia, and we were having difficulty communicating with him by phone or text. His e-mail replies were slow and incomplete, but we began to piece the information together.

During the signing of the scroll, the bottom section reserved for signatures quickly became full, as the numerous signatories embraced the spirit of John Hancock and signed their names large enough for our senator to read without his spectacles. This left only the space between the body of our letter and the edge of the scroll itself to sign. That was fine enough, but one individual took it upon himself to sign his name in the space between two paragraphs, and it was not his name that he signed but rather his nickname. None of us on the committee had noticed this, and it was not caught until fifteen hours before the scheduled delivery.

The offender was a veteran who had earned his nickname in the military. It was a play on words based on his last name and his toughness as a soldier. Everyone referred to him by his nickname, and he had used it for the past forty years. We could absolutely not deliver the scroll without the FBI and every other law enforcement agency coming after us. The maker of the scroll worked with our courier to see about removing the signature with rubbing alcohol and other agents, but to no avail. The John-Hancock-sized word *Killer* could not be removed, and the centerpiece of our media event the next morning was ruined.

I, along with many of the committee members, was livid. What person, nickname or not, would be blind to the fact that this would be a problem, unless it was an intentional act of sabotage? This individual was not on our list of registered attendees but had been allowed into the event nonetheless. The next several days saw an e-mail war for and against this individual, and I was very vocal about my displeasure with him and the incalculable damage that he had caused.

We had to salvage this in the best way we could, and that involved making a fancy, standard-paper-sized replica of our scroll. It would lessen the media impact of the scroll as a symbol, but we were running out of time.

At 9:00 a.m. on Monday, January 24, 2011, our courier, retirement letter in hand, met up with the DC area Tea Party, Tea Party Express, and CNN outside Senator Lugar's Washington offices. The entourage was greeted with surprise from a Lugar staff member who read the letter as the cameras rolled. The staffer was a bit taken aback by the contents of the letter but was gracious in accepting it and promised to deliver it to the senator. CNN's political ticker ran the story that morning. Mission accomplished.

Our efforts to garner media attention were far more successful than we could ever have imagined, and our story was about to go viral. CNN's coverage of the delivery of the retirement letter spawned hundreds of mentions of it around the nation. The Associated Press's coverage of our unity meeting appeared in newspapers in dozens of cities. The first interview request after our event came on Wednesday, January 26, from television station WTHR 13 in Indianapolis. I was asked to appear in their studios for comment on our efforts to retire Lugar. This would be the first of many interviews. It aired on the station's noon, six, and eleven o'clock editions; it featured footage of both me and Senator Lugar and ended with me climbing into my pickup truck with its Tea Party bumper stickers and driving away. We had received prime-time news coverage in the city of Indianapolis, former home of prodigal son and former mayor Dick Lugar—talk about taking the fight to the belly of the beast.

Day after day, the media requests poured in. We were interviewed by CQ Roll Call, the *New York Times*, Politico, the *Washington Post*, Fox News, CNN, the Associated Press, the *Indianapolis Star*, the *Kokomo Tribune*, Sydney Radio in Australia, and dozens of other outlets. This media frenzy propelled the unified Hoosiers for a Conservative Senate and its mission onto the national political scene. It made our senatorial race national and put Senator Lugar once again on the defensive. It also sowed the seeds for a smear campaign.

Senator Lugar had decided that his tactic for dealing with the Tea Party challenge would be to mock and ridicule us. Unlike another RINO that faced a Tea Party challenge in 2012, Orrin Hatch, who tried to court the Tea Party, Lugar called the Tea Party losers in society who were bitter about how things had worked out for them. Bitter? Heck yes, we were bitter, because the real losers were destroying our nation and making it increasingly difficult for tens of millions of people to make ends meet. Lugar was partially responsible for our nation's woes, and he added insult to injury by mocking us.

In early February, Fox News's Steve Brown called Monica and asked for comment on Lugar's recent remarks telling the Tea Party, and specifically Hoosiers for a Conservative Senate, to "get real." Lugar was defending his sponsorship of the START Treaty, one of many votes the Tea Party took issue with. Monica asked me for input, and I penned a letter in response and was stunned that Fox printed it in its entirety. The letter was from my hand, but Monica was given credit for it by Brown, and his headline read, "Lugar to Tea Party: 'Get Real'; Tea Party to Lugar: 'Get Lost.'"

Senator Lugar,

If you would like to see what real is, then come home once in a while and listen to real people rather than stubbornly refusing to leave not only the Beltway but the 1980s as well.

In the nearly thirty-six years that you have been in Washington, America and the world has witnessed great change. When you were first elected to the Senate in 1976, the Ford Pinto was in the news and the USSR was America's only real global adversary. Today, Ford is the only true American automobile manufacturer left standing, and America's enemies have grown to include not only the former USSR but China, North Korea, Iran, Syria, and a host of other countries that sponsor radical Islamic terrorism.

It seems that you, senator, are the one who needs to get real by not worrying about your misguided legacy of pretending to make the world safer. America is safe when she is strong. Our nuclear arsenal and military superiority are what ensure our freedom and safety.

The START Treaty cripples America and does nothing to address Russia's nearly ten thousand tactical nuclear warhead superiority. It also does nothing to address the nuclear weapons of China, North Korea, and Iran. During the Cold War years, America and the USSR both valued survival, and that, coupled with equivalent capability of annihilating the other, provided a powerful deterrent.

Today's world is far different from the one you stubbornly cling to. North Korea and Iran do not value survival the way America and the former USSR do. China's intentions are unknown, but its military threat is not.

The people of Indiana, like those in all of the heartland of America, are real in the sense that we worry about our future and that of our children. We realize that nearly all of America's problems have been brought about by career politicians on both sides of the aisle who have forgotten not only who they serve but also the oath they took to uphold and defend the Constitution of the United States of America.

Mr. Lugar, it is time for you to come home.

The Hoosiers for a Conservative Senate committee had unanimously given Monica and me complete authority to deal with the press, realizing that the news has a short shelf life and timeliness of response is critical. We were also given the authority to make on-the-spot judgment calls on all other issues if the board could not be reached for input in a timely manner. Getting the entire committee to respond to an e-mail within twenty-four hours was an ongoing problem, as some simply did not make checking their e-mail a priority.

My published letter to Lugar incensed two of our committee members. One member, in particular, did not want us to work with the media, saying that it was usually best to work quietly and not make a lot of noise. This person's logic was that we should not let them see us coming. I thought that this was an extremely shortsighted and flawed idea. The Tea Party movement of Indiana was not going to win this fight without help. This was an all-out war that we were waging, not only against an individual but against an entrenched political machine. They would not roll over and die without a fierce fight. David's sling needed a ballistic-tipped rock if he was to bring down Goliath. That weapon was not yet in the arsenal of the Tea Party and would only be made available if we made a lot of noise and proved that the giant was in for a fall.

Our dissenting committee member was not the only one to become irritated with the intense media coverage our grassroots army was gaining. We had put Senator Lugar in a near-constant defensive posture, but the empire was readying a counterattack, and they had an unlikely ally ready to strike as well.

Peter the Not Great was on the march.

CHAPTER 8

———— ◆ ————

Tribal Wars: Attack of the Hyenas

As our story continued to receive media coverage in the weeks following the unification of the Tea Party movement, we began to put our plan to work. We recruited Tea Party members to start work on a procedure for vetting candidates and a caucus plan. There were others working on compiling Lugar's long voting record and disseminating it to the public through a campaign of letters to the editor. The state was abuzz with grassroots activities, and our optimism ran high. We could not begin to work on the candidate education portion of our plan until there were candidates to step up to challenge Lugar.

The first candidate to do that was State Treasurer Richard Mourdock. His candidacy was announced on February 22, 2011, in Indianapolis. Mourdock was in his second term as state treasurer and had enjoyed large margins of victory in his two elections to the position. He also enjoyed wide Tea Party support. That same day, Peter the Not Great and his group issued a press release endorsing Mourdock. They reveled in proclaiming that they had thoroughly vetted Mourdock in the past and that they were the first Tea Party group to back him in the Senate race. They encouraged other groups to follow suit and discontinue their participation in Hoosiers for a Conservative Senate. No consideration of the possibility of other candidates entering the race or of the absolute need for backing only one candidate was mentioned.

We fielded only a handful of inquiries over the next few weeks from Tea Party leaders on whether Hoosiers for a Conservative Senate should endorse Mourdock. We were beginning to sense that Peter the Not Great was not content with being on the outside looking in and would continue to try to undermine our initiative. The few groups that questioned the continued need for Hoosiers for a Conservative Senate were assured that our plan was sound and that it needed to be carried to completion.

We were also making plans with FreedomWorks to cohost a three-day educational and training event in Indianapolis from March 24 to March 26. This was a significant boost for us, as it once again illustrated the muscle and clout that our unity was building. FreedomWorks' commitment to fund and conduct a three-day event spoke volumes about their belief in the strength of the organization we were building. We should have known that our optimism and hope for quick success would run into a cold dose of reality.

In early March, Hoosiers for a Conservative Senate received a call from the Japanese Embassy in Washington, DC. They were flying into Indianapolis on official business and wanted to meet with Monica and me afterward. Wow, the Japanese wanted to talk with us. They said they were interested in the Tea Party and wanted to know more about it. It seemed to me that I had heard that statement once before. Indeed I had, from Steven the Snake. Monica was very excited about this, and as with nearly all the media that Hoosiers for a Conservative Senate was garnering, she posted it on her Facebook page. I was skeptical and cautious about this proposed meeting; after all, as foreign diplomats, the Japanese had diplomatic immunity. Who knew what their intentions were? I did not want to go blindly into this meeting. I consulted with someone who had conducted a great deal of research on Lugar. He was adamant that I not attend the meeting, believing it was an assassination attempt. His reasoning was that Lugar was a globalist, had ties to the Fabian Society as a Rhodes Scholar, and held membership in the Council on Foreign Relations and other socialist groups. I was not as fearful as he, but I eventually decided not to attend the meeting in order to appease my friend. Monica wanted to grant the meeting, so as a precaution I urged her to bring along a friend and to meet during the day in a well-populated area. She met with the Japanese diplomat, and they discussed the approximately two hundred businesses that Japanese companies and individuals had invested in in our state and how Senator Lugar was instrumental in securing many of those deals. The bottom line was that they did not like change and were afraid that we were about to upset their apple cart. We will never know for sure, but I am convinced that Lugar or the Indiana State GOP told the Japanese that we were a threat to the status quo. First a billionaire, and now the Japanese were after us; what more could happen?

The three-day event that we were cohosting with FreedomWorks received extensive publicity and promotion through the power of FreedomWorks' media relations efforts and 1.5 million followers. One of the events we planned was a press conference in the capitol rotunda with Governor Mitch Daniels, Dick Armey, and others. Armey was to present Daniels with an award for his fiscal conservatism. We asked several key allies to participate in the press conference both as a reward and to build alliances. After Daniels was presented his award, former House Majority Leader and FreedomWorks Chairman Dick Armey publicly announced that FreedomWorks supported Daniels's speculated presidential run. This further incensed an already agitated Hoosiers for a Conservative Senate committee member who did not support Daniels because he was only a fiscal and not a social conservative. I had asked this board member to be a part of the press conference, and she was grateful to have been included, but afterward she left angry and did not return to participate in the remaining two days of the event.

On the last day of our FreedomWorks event, a *Wall Street Journal* reporter that I had met in February and had regular communication with came to Indianapolis to cover our weekend efforts against Lugar. He partially quoted Monica on our willingness to do the difficult work that would be required to defeat a six-term RINO. The butchered quote came out as, "We are ready to get our knuckles bloody." Later in the day, this same reporter attended an event seventy-five miles north that was being held by one of the toxic trio. This individual was the most vitriolic of the trio and had become known as the Wicked Witch of White County.

The Witch had issued a barrage of e-mails following our December breakfast meeting with Lugar demanding that we explain how we had the authority to meet with Senator Lugar and why we had not invited the entire Tea Party. Despite her contempt for us, she did attend our unity meeting in January. The day following the meeting in Tipton, the Witch issued an e-mail proclamation that her group was resigning from Hoosiers for a Conservative Senate, claiming that no unity was achieved and that Monica and I were trying to claim leadership over the Tea Party. Resigning from Hoosiers for a Conservative Senate was puzzling, as I do not remember there being an official sign-up or requirement for being part of our organization. Call me a cynic once again, but I thought the Witch was up to something.

Now the Witch went a step further by hosting the senator at a meeting with her group. This was the most destructive thing any Tea Party leader had ever done in the state—giving the senator a Tea Party audience after it had been universally agreed that he should retire. Now the *Wall Street Journal* was reporting on her meeting. We were sure Lugar would spin this in the media for all it was worth, claiming that he had the support of many Tea Party members. The following Monday, the *Wall Street Journal* article mentioned our three-day event, Monica's twisted quote, and the Witch's ill-conceived Lugar forum.

A day after Monica's quote appeared in public, the producer of the Fox News show *Your World with Neil Cavuto* called to request that we appear on Cavuto's show. Monica's misquoted words had piqued the producer's interest in our Senate battle, and she saw a good story in the making. This exciting news immediately found its way onto Monica's Facebook page, but the excitement was short-lived; the Witch was about to hit the fan.

Peter the Not Great, his partner Sooie, and the Wicked Witch of White County launched an extensive smear campaign against Monica and me out of nothing more (I surmised) than petty jealousy. On Tuesday, March 29, 2011, a scathing e-mail campaign began with a message to the statewide movement, the media, Fox News, and Cavuto. In the e-mail were allegations of wrongdoing by Hoosiers for a Conservative Senate and of threats and disrespect toward Senator Lugar; the mangled quote about bloody knuckles was given as an example. They continued their tirade with assertions that we were claiming leadership of the Tea Party. The final assault was led by the Witch, who claimed there was a questionable relationship between Monica and me. All three wrote long e-mails full of fallacious allegations and publicized them.

My phone rang within minutes of the e-mail being sent, and Monica was incredulous. She informed me of the e-mail release and was stunned at the level of hatred the three had displayed. In the e-mails, I was referred to as Monica's sidekick. Peter the Not Great was so blinded by his rivalry with Monica that he dismissed me as not having much of a role in the success of Hoosiers for a Conservative Senate. I was relegated in status to a mere tagalong, whereas Monica was the primary target of his hatred. The Witch, on the other hand, had no problem attacking in an equitable fashion.

We were shocked and worried about how the media and the statewide movement would receive this attack. It was obviously extremely unprofessional and smacked of a smear campaign, but would others see it that way? Two days later, Peter the Not Great took it a step further by appearing on an Indianapolis radio talk show to explain his attacks on us by saying that the Tea Party, a bottom-up movement, was not to be controlled by any one organization and that Hoosiers for a Conservative Senate was trying to run the Tea Party. This was an intentional misrepresentation of the truth about the structural setup of Hoosiers for a Conservative Senate, but Peter was not above trying to present himself as a righteous savior whose only concern was rushing in to save the Tea Party from impending doom. The host of this radio show had been invited to our Tipton meeting. He was controversial and enjoyed bashing the Tea Party. He reported several times that his sources—which was code for himself—told him that FreedomWorks was concerned about Hoosiers for a Conservative Senate's ability to organize. That was laughable, because my sources—by which I mean me—told me that FreedomWorks remained committed to working with us, and nobody in Indiana had closer ties with FreedomWorks than

I did. When asked by the radio host to comment on what Peter had said, I paraphrased Ronald Reagan's eleventh commandment to say that I would not speak ill of fellow Tea Party members. What was actually reported was that I had no comment. I immediately contacted the radio show host about his unfair reporting, and he agreed to have me in the studio the following Monday. After careful deliberation I declined the invitation, believing my participation would only further extend the story.

Late on the afternoon of Peter, Sooie, and the Witch's combined assault on us, a blogger came to our defense. When I opened the link to his article about this upsetting war of words, I nearly fell out of my chair with laughter. The Angry White Boy blog had published the beginning of what would become a four-part series called "There's a Turd in the Tea Party Punch Bowl." That turd was Peter the Not Great, and contained within the story were the e-mail letters that the trio had sent out. Total public discredit was rightfully placed on the turd and his accomplices. The smear campaign, at least for now, was squelched, and the casualties were few. Cavuto's producer never did follow through with her offer, and we received and accepted the resignation of our media-shy board member, who had had enough of the media drama.

We vowed to press on. We were tired, scathed, and thirsty, but we were not about to draw a cup of refreshment from that punch bowl.

CHAPTER 9

———— ◆ ————

Swatting Mosquitoes

Believing that we had weathered the storm of the smear campaign and clear skies lay ahead, the Hoosiers for a Conservative Senate committee got down to the task of following through with our plan. At this point, we had lost the representatives of the second, sixth, and ninth districts and had never had a representative for the first district. Monica's original pick for district two had decided that she no longer had the stomach for Peter the Not Great's attacks. District six was vacated by our media-weary representative, and district nine opened with the appointment of our representative to a county GOP chairmanship—a clear conflict of interest, as the representative acknowledged in his resignation.

We were five months into our mission, and we had been verbally attacked by Lugar, approached with a bribe from a billionaire, checked out by the Japanese, and smeared by the toxic trio. The experience was taking its toll, and we were operating at half strength in committee personnel. Our original district two representative recommended her replacement, and we found another Tea Party activist to represent district six. The first district had no representative until September, and we finally found a representative for the ninth district four months after the original representative resigned.

Monica and I threatened to quit many times, although never seriously. When one of us felt down, the other always seemed ready to offer words of encouragement. My favorite means of coaxing Monica back into the fight and motivating myself was the analogy of a fallen warrior reaching down and picking up his sword, climbing back onto his horse, and fighting on. I hate to lose, despise quitters, and am a very poor sport. Call it stubbornness or stupidity, but losing was not an option. We were not going to allow Lugar and his surrogates or the toxic trio to win without an all-out fight. Apparently our adversaries did not get the memo, and Lugar launched yet another salvo in our direction, this time aimed squarely at Monica and Richard Mourdock.

Lugar's official campaign spokesman, Mark Helmke, fired the shot in the form of an e-mail: "In the past several months, a Warsaw, Indiana, college secretary named Monica Boyer has received incredible national press coverage for her attacks on Senator Dick Lugar. Google reports that 'Monica Boyer Indiana' has 1,530,000 hits. Impressive, especially when compared to the declared primary candidate against Lugar, Richard Mourdock, with 26,400 hits."

Helmke had inadvertently exposed himself and his boss as the endangered, out-of-touch species that they were. He did not understand the internet or what constituted a Google hit. Helmke had incorrectly performed his search in a way that returned every page with any of his three search terms—*Monica*, *Boyer*, or *Indiana*. The proper method of conducting this search would have been to include a plus sign between each term. Using this proper search produced only 9,770 hits. Richard Mourdock in quotation marks resulted in 46,100 results.

Lugar and his agents were more intent on attacking Hoosiers for a Conservative Senate than they were on attacking their only declared primary challenger, Richard Mourdock. Helmke went on to try to discredit Monica by stating, "Last November, Monica Boyer lost a three-way race for the Warsaw school board 65 to 19 to 17. Seventeen votes for Monica from her neighbors, not the national media. And then, just yesterday, Monica's husband was on the ballot in the Republican Primary for the Warsaw City Council District 2. Brian Boyer lost 135 to 70."

The empire had been reduced to launching attacks on their own constituents through bribe attempts, insults, and ridicule. The bigger they are …

Our district two seat was filled for only a short length of time. The new representative was practically neighbors with Peter the Not Great and felt that he could play him in order to gather intelligence and make peace. He attended Peter and Sooie's meetings and was also in communication with the Witch. Through him, we learned of a competing event that the toxic trio was planning to counter the caucus that we had planned for later that fall.

Hoosiers for a Conservative Senate had originally planned on conducting a caucus to vet candidates and narrow down an anticipated field of candidates to one that the Tea Party could rally behind and support. Our caucus committee was formulating a plan for conducting the caucus, and their report caused much internal strife. Many in the Tea Party did not want to be perceived as being part of the Republican Party, so they demanded total objectivity in the caucus process. The caucus committee recommended that all of the senatorial candidates, including the Democrat, be invited to our caucus. Only the district two representative agreed with this suggestion, and dissension once again ran through the committee. The district two and district four representatives verbally sparred over this issue, which led to the district two representative's eventual resignation. At issue was whether we were being objective in only inviting Republican candidates to our caucus. The majority of the board felt that our original goal as defined in our mission statement was to defeat Senator Lugar and replace him with a true conservative and that this could only be achieved by beating him in the Republican primary. No Democrat was going to be conservative and, in any case, no Democrat was going to run in the Republican primary, so inviting a Democrat to our caucus seemed pointless.

We were navigating through difficult and uncharted territory and feeling the toll. There was internal strife in our committee, a restless Tea Party waiting for marching orders, and the toxic trio plotting additional blows. It was now early May, and many were advocating for Hoosiers for a Conservative Senate to hold the caucus in June. Lugar still had Richard Mourdock as his lone challenger, and the anticipated decision from State Senator Delph continued to be pushed back. Delph had promised an announcement at the conclusion of the spring legislative session, but when it passed, he further delayed his decision.

If we caved to the pressure and consented to having a June caucus, we risked the possibility of other candidates getting into the race later, causing the Tea Party groups to renege on their pledge of supporting the candidate chosen in the caucus and jump ship to another. June was too early to push for a caucus; it was eleven months before our May 8, 2012, primary and eight months before the last filing date to declare candidacy. We had the luxury of time to do this right, but we did not have the luxury of patient collaborators.

The toxic trio was hard at work during this challenging period, and their sinister plans were soon made public. On June 11, in Kokomo, Indiana, they would be hosting a rally called "It's Real Tea Time, Indiana," and Treasurer Mourdock was to be the guest of honor. The Wicked Witch of White County contacted Monica and me to say that it was time to put our differences aside and attend their rally. The Witch stated that both sides were guilty of the rift and pleaded for our attendance. Monica engaged with her briefly in conversation, but I refused to reply to any of her dozens of e-mails. She had never admitted to or apologized for the false allegations the trio had made, and until she did, I was not going to fall for her disingenuous offers of reconciliation.

We also took issue with their use of the word *real*, believing that it was a veiled insinuation either that they spoke for Hoosiers for a Conservative Senate or that Hoosiers for a Conservative Senate was somehow illegitimate. When others asked them for an explanation, they claimed to have gotten the idea of using the word *real* from a conversation with Governor Daniels. The Witch said that the governor had suggested that the Tea Party movement was real and that she should use the word as a campaign slogan for Richard Mourdock. The funny thing about that claim was that Daniels was known for his contempt for the Tea Party and was a staunch Lugar supporter, having gotten his political start from him. The word *real* was being used deceptively to suggest that they were the real Tea Party organization and that the caucus was being held in Kokomo on June 11. If Monica and I had attended, we would have fallen for their deception. The Witch had overplayed her hand by insisting that Monica and I bury the hatchet by attending this event—the same hatchet she had buried in our backs only weeks earlier.

It occurred to me that perhaps it was time to employ a rope-a-dope strategy—the maneuver made famous by Muhammad Ali in his fight with George Foreman. The trio had been swinging wildly at us for weeks with most blows not landing on their intended targets. We would allow them to continue to do so until it was time to strike a solid and decisive blow on them.

Once again, we were presented with another challenge that we had neither the time nor the patience for. Defeating Lugar was the mission at hand, and these distractions were wasting valuable time. We prayed that the unusually wet spring would continue at least through their event and asked God for deliverance. Then, as if our prayers had been answered, Mike Pence announced plans to hold his gubernatorial campaign launch in Columbus on June 11. Mike Pence entered the picture once again, and at least for one day I could confidently say, "I like Mike."

This announcement was sweet music to our ears, for Pence would be sure to attract hundreds of Tea Party activists to his kickoff event, which would hurt the turnout at the toxic trio's event. Monica, an ardent Pence supporter, traveled to Columbus along with a few hundred other people that June Saturday. I, on the other hand, had something much more clandestine planned. We had primed our nemesis for a knockout punch, and I was determined to deliver it. I would be heading to Kokomo to keep a certain group real—as in honest. This group would undoubtedly promote their event as a raving success and claim that the whole Tea Party was in support of them. I had no choice but to take the position and stance of a sniper. There was a nice high vantage point at the adjoining property from which I could begin assessing the layout of the event. Where was everybody? There were more flags displayed than there were people. Including the speaking guests and vendor booth attendees, I arrived at a count of fifty people at what was promoted as the real Tea Party event complete with thousands of Hoosiers participating. Completion of Operation Rope a Dope would be swift. I was hidden from view between the cars of two Taco Bell customers. Peering into my sights and adjusting for wind speed, temperature, and relative humidity, I gently squeezed the trigger and ripped off dozens of rounds of photographs. My chip full, I immediately began downloading my reconnaissance evidence onto several social media sites. A picture speaks a thousand words, and nothing further needed to be said about the "real" Tea Party group. The Tea Party movement in Indiana could see for themselves. I sent a report of the completed covert operation to Monica in Columbus, and she responded with incredulity. Mission accomplished: the enemy was neutralized.

Given enough rope, the toxic trio had pounded relentlessly on us. In the end, the real dopes hanged themselves.

CHAPTER 10

———◆———

Keeping an Eye on the Prize

It was now time to brush off the distractions and get back to the business of defeating longtime RINO Senator Richard Lugar. A few Tea Party groups, Mourdock supporters, and the media were all clamoring for us to conduct our caucus in June. Turning a deaf ear to this chorus, we remained resolute in following our plan to fruition, and that meant not bowing to the immense pressure we were feeling. We knew that the summer months were the doldrums for political campaigns and that if we held the caucus now, the media and public would lose interest soon afterward, and then it would be a long, lonely way to the primary. We were already beginning to notice a sharp drop in media interest in our story, and keeping them asking about our caucus seemed a good way to keep our story alive. This was just one of the factors in our logic; the continued speculation about additional challengers entering the race was another one that weighed heavily.

Hoosiers for a Conservative Senate had grown to the point of nearly being a full-time job for us—one with long hours and lousy pay. I joked with Monica whenever we had a particularly good day that I was doubling her pay. Twice zero is still zero, but the laughter we derived from the joke seemed to propel us a little farther down the road. All of the committee members had full-time jobs and families to attend to, but Monica and I always had to be on call and available to respond to the ever-growing demands placed on us.

Our frustrations about the impossibility of being all things to all people were growing. Many in our coalition felt that Hoosiers for a Conservative Senate was communicating too much with the various Tea Party groups, while others complained about a lack of communication. There was a constant struggle to hold the coalition together as we worked on our plan, fought off attacks, and trudged on toward the fall and our caucus. We finally decided to send out a weekly e-mail to our groups to keep them informed on the progress toward our goal as well as to offer words of encouragement. Our newsletter promoted our plan and the phase we were in at any particular time and praised the success of individual groups. Many groups were involved in letter-to-the-editor campaigns, voter data research, and recruitment. Most Tea Party groups around the state had made it their primary focus to defeat Senator Lugar. They were still involved in other conservative issues, but Lugar's defeat was on the top of the list.

Our research committee, assigned the task of gathering Lugar's extensive voting record, collapsed under the weight of the task. They decided that a simpler approach was needed, and the new strategy quickly produced online downloadable data. We shared this data with all the Tea Party groups for use in educating the public on Lugar's liberal voting record. Many groups pulled voter information from their county elections boards and began door-to-door campaigns to educate people about Lugar's record with verifiable data in hand. An organized and coordinated effort was slowly beginning to take shape.

In addition to all this effort, some of the Hoosiers for a Conservative Senate district representatives held regular meetings with the Tea Party groups located in their districts. There were twelve Tea Party groups in my district, and we promoted ourselves as the strongest and most dedicated of any of the districts in an attempt to encourage others to follow our lead. Monica and I set up competing Facebook pages for our districts, and the rivalry served as motivation for the groups to outperform one another.

On June 14, the e-mail wars started again with an accusation from a member of Peter the Not Great's group. He said that he was beginning to see a trend in the state Tea Party movement of one group boycotting another group's events and encouraging others to do the same. On the heels of the poorly attended It's Real Tea Time Indiana rally, this individual was accusing Hoosiers for a Conservative Senate of boycotting the event. We had not boycotted it or encouraged others to do so; we had merely chosen not to participate in an event hosted by deceptive people that did not contribute to the goal of defeating Lugar. This allegation prompted responses both from Hoosiers for a Conservative Senate supporters and our old friend the Witch and her few followers. It was obvious that they were reeling from the public exposure of their unsuccessful rally and the harm it had caused the Mourdock campaign. It was time to lay blame elsewhere, and we were their favorite punching bag.

The Witch jumped into the cyber fray by making the ridiculous accusation that Hoosiers for a Conservative Senate had influenced Congressman Pence to hold his campaign launch on the same day as their rally. The Witch was actually publicly stating that we had the influence to get a congressman to host an event on a day that we chose. Our influence was indeed growing, but not to the point that we could sway a gubernatorial candidate to help us in our efforts, especially since those efforts were counter to the goals of the GOP establishment of which Pence was a part. I was amused at that, but as the day went on, the charges and accusations mounted. Up until this point in our seven-month existence, I had suppressed the desire to respond in an e-mail war of words. But I had had about all I could take of the Wicked Witch and her cohort, and I was ready to call her out.

I first explained why, in my opinion, their rally was such an abject failure. Their boastful claims that several thousand people would be attending were not believable, and it undermined their already poor credibility. They also failed to do any promotion of the event and lacked basic skills in marketing. No consideration was given to the fact that the day for mass rallies in the movement had passed; the movement had matured and settled into the task of doing the hard work of effecting change, and that was not to be achieved by rallying; nor was it an effective use of money and man hours. My explanation of why their event had failed was met with even more furor. The Wicked Witch of White County possessed the juvenile trait of never being able to let someone else have the last word. After every response, no matter how well thought out and decisively convincing, the Witch replied hastily with mumbo-jumbo vitriol. She proclaimed that she had tried to bury the hatchet for the good of the cause. I reminded her that she had never apologized for the inexcusable and false accusations she had made against Monica and me. She replied unconvincingly that we all shared blame for the war and that she was merely trying to move forward, and that Monica and I were the cause of any divisiveness. I reminded her of her allegations of an improper relationship between Monica and me. She stated that she had only meant we had a questionable business arrangement. Unable to squelch her rhetoric completely, I decided to call her out by republishing her smear campaign e-mail letter from the previous March, complete with the allegation of an improper relationship. This was news to most participating in this current e-mail war and led one Tea Party member and former district two representative to say, "That's what I like about you, Greg; you play with all your cards facing up." The Witch was knocked off her broomstick once more, but I was sure that she had others waiting in her closet. She and her minions proclaimed that two could play the boycott game—never mind that we had not boycotted their rally—and threatened to disrupt our planned caucus.

In late June I attended FreedomWorks' Boot Camp 2.0, campaign training weekend in Washington, along with 150 other activists from around the nation. The three-day session was designed to give us the information and training we would need for the 2012 election season. I could not wait to mingle with my peers and tell them what we were doing in Indiana. My credibility with FreedomWorks was rising with the success of Hoosiers for a Conservative Senate. I had been in close correspondence with members of their staff since January, and we were on track to win their endorsement of our candidate at some point after our caucus. Our strategy was paying off and being recognized, and it felt good.

One of the first training sessions FreedomWorks conducted that weekend was on Saturday, June 25, and it concerned the political landscape of the nation. Projected up on their screen was a color-coded map of the United States with each state highlighted. It was a battle map of the plan for retaking the US Senate. The states that had Senate races in play in 2012 were colored to show whether they were currently held by a Republican or a Democrat. The strategy was to pick up as many Democratic held seats as possible. Indiana was colored red for Republican, a zero net gain in the quest for retaking the Senate.

I was anxious for the anticipated announcement that although Indiana's senatorial race would not spell a net gain in the US Senate, FreedomWorks would be helping Hoosiers for a Conservative Senate to elect someone to that seat more in the image of conservative Senators Mike Lee, Marco Rubio, and Jim DeMint. *Here it comes, our great story of statewide Tea Party unity in Indiana.* This would be sweet validation of our hard work.

Indiana indeed was mentioned. FreedomWorks would not be focusing their attention on our race but instead was looking at the Senate race in Utah. I was stunned. Numbness paralyzed my thought. Whiskey tango foxtrot. Whatcha talkin 'bout Willis? I barely heard any more of the conversation about the Senate race strategy other than something about limited resources. This weekend was really going to stink.

FreedomWorks' involvement was a key piece of the strategy I had formulated. I had all but promised the Hoosiers for a Conservative Senate committee their commitment to our cause. We had made our race a national race through our media contacts. We had done the nearly impossible and unified the movement, and even that wasn't enough. What more did we have to do? What more did I have to do?

My relationship with FreedomWorks had first started with my participation in their Liberty Leadership Summit in January 2010. In what I can only explain as Providence, I received an e-mail invitation to attend this exclusive gathering of sixty of the top activists from around the country. I should not have been invited to be part of such an accomplished group; I had been flying under the radar within the movement at this point. I do not even know how FreedomWorks could have gotten my name or e-mail address, but there it was—an invitation that may very well have sealed the fate of one of the biggest RINOs ever to roam the American heartland. I was off to Washington, DC, for the third time in four months, and this visit was to be more important than any before or later.

Of all the valuable lessons FreedomWorks taught me, none stayed with me longer or was bitterer to swallow than the one that Hoosier Tea Party activists forced upon themselves. Our unorganized efforts in the 2010 elections resulted in only a few thousand yard signs, compliments of FreedomWorks, for three of our nine congressional districts.

There were many rewards to reap from unity, and our nation's survival counted on it. If the Tea Party was going to save America, it needed to understand that it had to work together in a cooperative and coordinated manner. When asked to deliver those few thousand signs for distribution, I asked why there were so few and was told that given the unorganized movement in the state, investment of resources was likely to yield little return.

I was about to be reminded of that long-ago battle cry of our founding fathers, "Unite or die."

CHAPTER 11

——◆——

He Who Laughs Last: Silencing the Hyenas

At the conclusion of the FreedomWorks session on the Senate race, I hurried out of the room determined to find out what had happened. One staff member told me that he was not totally sure why they were no longer looking at Indiana. Another gave me a similar story but provided some detail. FreedomWorks' economist said we live in a world of limited resources and, as such, those resources need to be allocated where there are the best chances of success. I pressed further, asking the staff members I knew best, and a picture started to emerge.

FreedomWorks was not going to get involved in our race because of concern about the dissension and lack of unity within the state movement. I had no idea what they were talking about. Other than not having the toxic trio included in our coalition, we were unified from Lake Michigan to the Ohio River. The only dissension was from Peter, Sooie, and the Witch. This was not right, so I continued to try to make sense of it all.

I finally got my answer. The smear campaign had never ended, and in fact it was in high gear. Sooie and the Witch had been placing numerous and regular calls to FreedomWorks, urging them to jump ship and join their coalition of three. They had promised that they would be holding a well-attended caucus in June. They had absolutely no idea how much damage they had done to their candidate and how little influence they held. Only a few weeks earlier, the Witch had mocked my efforts to secure the help of FreedomWorks, stating that we—meaning the Tea Party—did not need them in our race and that they would come running to us. Now they were courting FreedomWorks in an effort to give their group legitimacy and to deceive the Tea Party into believing the caucus was being held in June. What they had not taken into consideration was that FreedomWorks did not necessarily share their belief that a caucus had to be held in June and no later; they also did not understand my relationship with the organization. Their deceptive and divisive actions were more than enough to convince FreedomWorks to question any claim of statewide unity. The toxic trio seemed to have single-handedly destroyed any chance of bringing down Lugar in the May 2012 primary. I was once again stunned at the level of malice, contempt, and pure jealousy that these three possessed, and I set out to salvage what I could from the wreckage.

That same weekend I received a call from State Senator Delph asking if I had heard the latest news about Mourdock. The Lugar campaign had made some allegations about him, but they had no merit and no legs. I had not heard about this situation, and the senator provided me with details and went on to ask me what the Tea Party would think of it. This politician was not one to make a social call, especially on a weekend, so I knew this call could only mean that he was still assessing his options for a Senate run. Peter and the Witch knew Monica and I were friends with this senator and were constantly alleging that we supported him and were stalling in order not to hold the caucus until he had made his decision.

On Monday, June 27, FreedomWorks held a press conference in their offices. Numerous media organizations came to hear about our campaign training and to follow a group of activists from Utah. Their offices were adorned with dozens of glossy, corrugated vinyl yard signs reading "Retire Hatch," and Utah Senator Mike Lee was going to be visiting that same morning. As my eyes scanned the offices, I began to formulate a plan. I sent a quick e-mail to the communications coordinator with the Mourdock campaign to request a meeting later in the week. This plan would require quick work and a certain amount of luck, but if successful the toxic trio finally would be cast out of our way—and possibly out of the Tea Party. I had to work deliberately and without distractions. Kate Zernike of the *New York Times* greeted me, having interviewed me before, and went to interview fellow activists. I then ran into *Wall Street Journal* reporter Danny Yadron. Yadron was the reporter I had first met at the CPAC conference the previous February in Washington, and he had attended our three-day event in Indianapolis. He asked me how our Senate race was going, and I strategically replied, "We don't have FreedomWorks." He asked why not, and I suggested that he ask FreedomWorks that question. That afternoon, Yadron's article ran in the *Wall Street Journal,* and it was exclusively about the Senate race in Indiana and FreedomWorks' noninvolvement:

> FreedomWorks, the conservative activist group that helped launch the Tea Party two years ago, hasn't yet decided if it will back a primary challenge against Sen. Richard Lugar (R., Ind.). "We're not going to climb the hill unless we have a reasonable shot at taking the hill," Adam Brandon, a FreedomWorks spokesman, told *Washington Wire* on Monday. Mr. Lugar, a top target for some conservatives, will face Indiana State Treasurer Richard Mourdock, a favorite of conservatives, in next year's primary. Back in March, a FreedomWorks delegation huddled with a group of Tea Party activists at an Indianapolis hotel to discuss strategy against Mr. Lugar. The fact that some of Mr. Lugar's Washington opponents are still undecided signals their concerns about Mr. Mourdock's chances of winning the general election.

The article may have seemed like bad news for the Mourdock campaign to some at the time, but it was actually the best thing that could have happened, and I was pleased.

I next grabbed a Retire Hatch sign and proceeded to the glass-enclosed conference room. Inside, Utah Senator Mike Lee was speaking to a group of his constituents, Tea Party activists who only the year before had been instrumental in electing him. I aimed my infamous camera at the senator and his audience and snapped a few pictures. I then returned to the main body of activists gathered around the press corps. They were discussing a plan to take the Retire Hatch signs over to the National Republican Senatorial Committee and demand that the NRSC stay out of the Utah Senate race and end its support of Hatch. Zernike overheard me telling someone of my plans while holding my Hatch sign, and later that day her article appeared in the *New York Times*. The last paragraph stated, "Greg Fettig, an activist from Indiana, was among those toting the 'Retire Hatch' placards. 'I'm going to take it home and get others,' he said, 'saying, "Retire Lugar."'"

There was only one thing left to accomplish for my plan to work, and that was to secure a meeting with the president of FreedomWorks, Matt Kibbe. Earlier in the weekend I had been told that Kibbe was aware of my frustrations and that he wanted to talk to me about it. It was the last day of the boot camp, and I would be flying home later that afternoon. To secure any time with Matt was difficult with his busy schedule, but to be able to do so on this day, with an office full of reporters conducting interviews and covering the NRSC event, was a godsend.

Matt invited me into his office, and we sat and talked for thirty minutes. I spoke of our accomplishments to date and the problems we were having. I also discussed our reasons for having the caucus in the fall and not earlier. I told Matt that we felt a great burden of responsibility to the Tea Party movement in Indiana not to be too hasty in rallying around a single candidate. If we did not thoroughly vet a candidate but rather jumped blindly into giving him our endorsement, we risked destroying our credibility as a movement. If it turned out after our endorsement that our candidate had some issue that would derail his campaign, our mission and credibility—and the credibility of the movement as a whole—would be destroyed, likely permanently. The weekend call from the state senator and the Lugar campaign's attempts to discredit the only announced candidate glaringly illustrated that point. This burden weighed heavily on me, and it was not one that I would set aside lightly.

We also discussed not only the politically righteous reasons for defeating both Lugar and Hatch but the shockwave it would create in the politics-as-usual establishment. Matt told me that they felt they had a better chance of beating Senator Hatch than Lugar. I responded by saying, "Why settle for one when we can have them both?" I promised him that we were committed to this goal and would remain so. Finally, he asked me what I wanted. I said that at the very minimum, I would like to have unlimited yard signs, door hangers, palm cards, and phone-bank systems for Tea Party use in support of our candidate. Matt told me about the FreedomWorks for America Super PAC that was being created and the financial possibilities that could come from it. His marching orders to me were to go back home and secure statewide Tea Party unity. He said if we could pull it all together, we would have their support in the end. This was the final piece to my plan—the news I needed to be able to take back home to Indiana in order to deliver a devastating knockout blow to the toxic trio.

I gathered up my Retire Hatch sign and headed to Reagan National Airport. The sign could not be folded or damaged in any way; it had to arrive home intact. As I sat at the gate waiting for my flight, several people passed by, read my sign, and gave me the thumbs-up sign. The overhead cargo bins were too small to contain my shiny carry-on, so I wedged it between the window seat and the fuselage. When refreshments were finally served, the flight attendant addressed me by asking, "What would our political activist like to drink?" He had absolutely no idea how right he was.

On Wednesday, June 29, I met with the manager and the communication director for the Mourdock campaign. Although I had spoken by phone with the communication director before, I had not met either of them. I was not sure how I would recognize them, but I knew they would know who I was if for no other reason than that I was carrying my Hatch sign. I was here meeting with them to complete my plan. After pleasantries were exchanged, I informed them of the mission of Hoosiers for a Conservative Senate and what we had accomplished thus far. They were fairly aware of what and who we were, as was their boss, Richard Mourdock. I had met with Mourdock at the CPAC conference in Washington several months earlier, where he had not only asked that I arrange a meeting for him with Tea Party Express but also had asked for my endorsement. Monica and I had also both met with him just a couple of weeks before in an effort to get him to silence the toxic trio; we had even given him copies of their slanderous e-mails.

Today's visit was no social call; it was business. I produced copies of the *Wall Street Journal* and *New York Times* articles, of which they were painfully aware. I showed them my photograph of Senator Mike Lee and his Tea Party constituents and told the story of how they had banded together to get Lee elected. Next, I mentioned my Retire Hatch sign and how it could have been and should have been a Retire Lugar sign. Then I told them how the toxic trio had cost their campaign hundreds of thousands of dollars by subverting our efforts to secure FreedomWorks' support of our candidate. Their jaws dropped in disbelief, and I suppressed a smile. I had them primed and more than receptive of my cure. They had to silence the toxic trio or I was done with Hoosiers for a Conservative Senate, and with my departure, any chance of FreedomWorks getting involved in the race would be lost. I knew that they wielded influence over the trio, given their early endorsement of Mourdock and their constant events and meetings in support of him. It was that simple—silence them now or we were done. The campaign manager said that he did not know if he could get them to behave, but I responded by saying that Mourdock himself could. They did not have to disassociate themselves completely from the trio—just silence them and curb their subversive behavior. If I saw one disparaging e-mail, any effort to boycott our caucus, any hint of undermining our efforts, it was over, and I would focus my efforts elsewhere. The communication director glanced again at my Hatch sign and asked what I was going to do with it. I replied, not entirely truthfully, that it was a souvenir. *Please, please,* I thought, *ask me if you can have it.* And then he did just that. Every time they looked at that sign in their campaign offices, it would serve as a bitter reminder of what their campaign could have had, should have had, and would have had if not for the petty and destructive actions of a few. Mission accomplished.

As I left the parking lot, I could not help but think about what Col. Paul Tibbets of the Enola Gay must have felt when he delivered his devastating payload and quickly climbed upward and away from the expected blast. Hope of a final knockout punch to end a brutally long war rested with the delivery of this new and devastating weapon. I prayed that a Fat Man of our own would not be necessary.

CHAPTER 12

———◆———

Iced Tea: Hot in Pursuit

The rockets' red glare and the bombs bursting in air gave all of us hope that our nemesis was no longer there. I was in a celebratory mood, and so were many in the Tea Party groups, jubilant at the prospect that the bomb I had dropped on the toxic trio might finally result in an end to the distractions. A small group of Hoosiers for a Conservative Senate committee members and other activists met on July 3 to capitalize on the smooth sailing it had finally provided. The holiday weekend meeting found us all very cognizant of what we were fighting for. Our independence could only be retained if we wrestled back control of power from those who stubbornly clung to it and returned it to its rightful owners: we the people.

The patriotic weekend's parades and pageantry filled us with pride and resolve and propelled the committee forward to do our part to wrest power from one person in particular. It was time to launch our summer campaign and continue to work toward the fall. Our hot, muggy summer had many Tea Party activists chilly about the prospect of outdoors activism; they preferred the cooler confines of their air-conditioned homes. It was going to take some effort to get them to warm to the idea of campaigning.

Monica had been encouraging the Tea Party groups to take advantage of the 4-H fairs every county in the state held in July as a venue for educating the public about Lugar's record. Her group had come up with the unique idea of achieving this goal by hosting a booth at her county fair called Blowing the Whistle on Lugar's Record. She had purchased hundreds of small red plastic whistles to give to the children of those who stopped at her booth and listened to her message. The booth display was complete with a cardboard cutout of Senator Lugar and information on his voting record. The red whistles were a big hit with the fair crowd and drew many dozens of voters into her booth. Other groups were conducting their own campaigns at their local fairs. Still more activists were marching in parades around the state. We got our first hint that our nemesis friends might have had their wrists slapped by the Mourdock campaign when they stopped marching for him in a few parades and instead marched for another candidate running for a different office. This was a big deal, since they had been very active in supporting him publicly. We were enjoying the calm and putting it to good use, no longer wasting time on them. Nevertheless, I could not help but think that perhaps the storm had not passed and we were merely in the eye of the hurricane. We struggled to keep the many groups' eyes on the brass ring and found ourselves competing with barbeques, boating, golfing, and the summer heat and humidity.

The Tea Party groups in district five met regularly throughout the summer in the Elks Club in Tipton and later at the Kokomo Public Library. We all sensed something none of us had considered when we started this endeavor eight months earlier: we were all becoming close friends. After our Saturday morning meetings, we would go out to lunch and socialize. The Miami County Tea Party even held a late-summer pig roast and invited all the other Tea Party groups to attend. Gone were the mistrust, territorial battles, and other rivalries that had kept us from working together and flexing our muscles as a unified political force. Many leaders were asked to speak at the meetings of other Tea Party groups.

Hoosiers for a Conservative Senate continued to hold semiregular meetings to plot strategies and float ideas in pursuit of our goal. We were now meeting in the Noblesville Library after having lost the use of our cozier quarters at the inn. Sadly, the Frederick-Talbott Inn closed its doors in early spring, falling victim to the hard economic times that the Obama administration was imposing on all of us. This served as yet another motivation for us to fight on.

The summer doldrums were affecting us all, even the Hoosiers for a Conservative Senate committee. It felt as if we were sitting dead in the water with distant shores in sight but out of reach. There were many rumblings throughout the Tea Party about whether a caucus was even necessary when only one challenger had announced his candidacy. The committee and I were insistent that it was, if for no other reason than to provide media coverage for our candidate in the form of a symbolic endorsement from the entire Tea Party. It was decided that we would have our event as planned but that it would be conducted in a convention-style format. We chose September 24, 2011, as the date and an old 1940s movie theater in Greenfield, Indiana, as the venue. The caucus portion of the event would not be held if no other challenger came forward before that date.

Even with a date set and a vague idea of how the September event would look, we had dozens of issues to address before our vision became reality. It was nearing the end of July, and we were nowhere close to being able to pull off a statewide convention in two months. An emergency meeting of the Hoosiers for a Conservative Senate committee was held, and I decided to take charge of the direction of this particular meeting. The outline of the meeting was sent to all committee members, and I was determined that this meeting would be very productive. The night before the Saturday morning meeting, I received an e-mail from Monica stating that one of the committee members wanted ten minutes to pitch a campaign advertising idea for Tea Party groups to use. This did not set well with me, but for the sake of a unified committee, I consented to the request.

That particular Saturday found me to be in a less-than-patient mood. The pressures of getting everything organized by late September were taking their toll. I was in no mood for distractions. This day would test my patience more than any other in all the months of our mission. I started the meeting with less than a full committee, which was becoming the norm as our mission entered its ninth month. After an introduction of the topics to be discussed, the committee member who had asked for ten minutes to speak took the floor. Ten minutes dragged into forty–five, I became increasingly agitated. His ideas would have been interesting on any day but this one. I felt that this was not the time to be discussing an advertising idea; our plans for the convention took precedence. Finally, his presentation ended and we could get on with the scheduled agenda.

The next order of business was the caucus and convention. Over the next two hours, we discussed the intricate details of the marquee event, which would symbolize the unity of our movement. The sweltering summer temperature outside paled in comparison to the heated discussions in our small library room. A lengthy and passionate discussion about the convention and whether any of the Tea Party groups in the state could even participate ensued. The committee member who had already held the floor for nearly an hour brought up the contentious matter of the tax-exempt status of the Tea Party groups. Since our inception as Hoosiers for a Conservative Senate, we had answered hundreds of questions about whether Tea Party groups could participate in any sort of political campaigning. Many groups were chartered as 501(c)(3)s and 501(c)(4)s. Some were 527s, and others had no legal identity whatsoever. Hoosiers for a Conservative Senate was one of the few in the latter category. We had decided that we did not need any legal recognition, as we planned on taking in no money and did not want to be bound by any federal restrictions limiting our freedom of speech. It was just what one would expect from a bunch of vocal activists intent on rocking the boat. Through our research into the matter, we had determined that all of the Tea Party entities could participate in any meeting and that all but the 501(c)(3)s could participate in a caucus or political convention.

The one committee member holding our meeting hostage was not convinced and would not allow the meeting to proceed until he was. Back and forth from one committee member to another the conversation went. Painstakingly, I tried to take it all in. The determined board member went so far as to float the idea of asking all the Tea Party groups in the state to change their tax-exempt status to 501(c)(4). I was nearly at my wits' end at the colossal waste of time this meeting had become. It was my meeting, and I was as far removed from the captain's helm as one could be. I objected to the claim that it would not take much to convince the dozens of groups to change their tax status, let alone to actually get them to do so in less than eight weeks. That objection and my reasoning for it were met with agreement from the other committee members and with one in particular. He and the agenda wrecker battled it out as I slipped into a glassy-eyed trance. Suddenly and without warning, an open palm hit the table and got everyone's attention.

"We are not going to pursue any of this talk of getting groups to change their status. It is never going to happen. Nor is it necessary," I proclaimed. "What we are going to do, however, is to hold a straw poll at our convention." The group looked at me attentively as I continued with my revelation. "The Tea Party groups will attend our convention and participate in a straw poll, and the winner of the straw poll will receive the endorsement of Hoosiers for a Conservative Senate." This format would allow all the groups to provide a tacit endorsement of our candidate without risking a violation of federal or state law by expressing a direct endorsement. The weight of Hoosiers for a Conservative Senate's endorsement would be immense, as its clout would be derived from the unified sentiment of dozens of Tea Party groups. The faces of the committee members expressed agreement with my revelation. We discussed this in further detail, and our meeting was back on track and heading full steam toward the fall convention.

CHAPTER 13

———◆———

RINO in the Crosshairs

The old movie theater fit perfectly with the idea of what the convention should look like that I had been carrying around for several weeks. I wanted it to truly look like a political convention—like the ones seen on television during presidential election years. It would be immensely effective to have patriotic banners and signs on poles identifying the various groups. This had the potential to be a huge publicity tool that would look great through the camera lenses of the media.

The committee set out to figure out how to pull this off. All our various talents were put to use in making this event a phenomenal success. We had no choice but to make sure that it was; everything was at stake. If we failed, our reputation, the relevancy of the Tea Party, and our candidate's viability could all evaporate. We must not fail.

The ideas and creativity flowed in from all the members of the committee as well as others involved in the task. One dedicated activist volunteered to prepare our PowerPoint presentation, and others chipped in to make signs, name tags, credential badges, and check-in lists. The facade of the theater was a great opportunity to showcase our event. There were two glass display cases that would house our playbills, and the semicircular marquee would provide high visibility and promotion of the convention to the media as well as those who traveled along the National Road.

There was still talk of the eerily silent toxic trio waging a boycott of our convention. The long summer also gave the perception that the Tea Party had lost interest in our mission. We had more than enough reason to be concerned about a poorly attended event. Every group in the state was contacted and encouraged to participate in this historic event that would display our unity and allow us to flex our collective muscles. We set September 6 as the final date for registration, and the requests for tickets trickled in. Ten days before the cutoff date, we received notice that the Tea Party of Hamilton County would be holding a competing event in a neighboring county. How could anyone in the Tea Party be so reckless as to host an event on the same day as the statewide convention—unless, of course, they were not a real Tea Party group. Suspicions mounted when we learned that Senator Lugar's political director and staff would be at the competing event. There were rumors that it was being sponsored by the county GOP. The offending group claimed to have been unaware of our event; apparently they were the only Tea Party group in the entire state not to know about the straw poll.

Days before the convention, we heard once again from the toxic trio; it seemed they had risen from the ashes of the nuclear blast. This time it was Peter the Not Great who released an e-mail stating that his group would not be participating in the Hoosiers for a Conservative Senate straw poll and convention. He claimed that his and all groups would be in violation of federal law if they attended due to the fact that FreedomWorks, a super PAC, would be in attendance. What he did not tell his audience was that FreedomWorks would be attending as a 501(c)(4), and as such, no group's legal status would be in jeopardy. Peter also did not mention that his group held no legal status and that he could attend without any risk of penalty. This deception prompted the Angry White Boy blog to publish part three of its series "There's a Turd in the Tea Party Punch Bowl." Once again, Peter was exposed for who he was. He would have been wise to remember the sage advice of Dirty Harry: "A man's got to know his limitations."

The deception, however, did not exclusively come from the toxic trio. We learned that the Lugar campaign was pulling out all the stops to deceive the public and trying to diminish both our movement and Hoosiers for a Conservative Senate. I was left speechless when an *Indianapolis Star* reporter called and asked if I was aware that our name and initials had been taken. Bewildered, I replied that I had not and she filled me in with the details. In mid-September, a former Lugar paid staffer (although we believed she was still working for the campaign), by her own admission, filed papers with the state claiming our name. When asked why she did so, she replied that she supported the Tea Party (yeah, right, and I have a bridge in Brooklyn for sale) but not their efforts to defeat the fine and conservative Senator Lugar. When I filed to reserve our name with the state, I had been unaware that the filing would be valid for only four months and that I would not be notified of its approaching expiration. So from June through September, our name was available, and then, coincidentally right before our convention, someone stole it. Yep, that bridge I have is a really good deal; are you interested? Now our name could be used by the Lugar camp to deceive the public in numerous ways. In a further act of desperation and deceit, Lugar's political director went around the state proclaiming that there were "different flavors of tea," falsely insinuating that the loyalty of grassroots organizations was split between the senator and Richard Mourdock. He backed up this statement by noting that the Witch had hosted the senator the previous March. This same individual, rumor had it, had set up a fake Tea Party group in his family's home in Rush County in eastern Indiana. We were to discover later that he was in direct contact with the group in Hamilton County. Not coincidentally, this fake Tea Party group from Rush County was made up of ardent Lugar supporters. Several days after our deadline for participation had passed, this group requested tickets to attend. Their request was denied; we explained that the deadline had passed and avoided a potential scene.

We were not convinced that our convention would not be undermined or disrupted. A bomb threat was called in to the Hendricks County Courthouse, which was just a block from the theater, only a few days before the convention. Some believed that this was the test run of a plan for stopping our festivities.

Both Senator Lugar and Richard Mourdock were invited to the convention, and both were given a list of thirty questions to answer as a means of vetting them for consideration by the straw poll delegates. The Mourdock campaign immediately accepted our invitation and supplied the answers to our questions. Senator Lugar did not respond to our invitation or answer our list of questions. It was our assumption that the second question had him worried; it asked for the respondent's address. Lugar would have been forced to respond with the Virginia address where he had lived for the past thirty plus years. CNN ran a story several days before our event stating that Lugar would not be attending and had said that the outcome was a foregone conclusion. Well, we had been fair; so much for there being different flavors of tea.

The night before the convention, two dozen activists conducted a dry run of the event and assigned duties. At the top of the list of concerns was security. As at the Tipton event, we hired a deputy sheriff to conduct security, but we aimed to allow no breach in our three-part sign-in process. Everybody allowed into the movie theater had to be preregistered. They also had to produce identification, sign next to their names on the printed list of preregistered attendees, and wear a wristband to show that they had signed in. Voting delegates would receive a different colored wristband than gallery observers, and everyone entering the theater portion of the building had to present their wristbands to the biggest guys we could find to man the doors. There was not going to be any trouble if we could help it.

Two hours before the event and one hour before the doors opened, the two dozen of us scampered around the ticket booth, stage, seating area, vestibule, and projection room. Each of us had a task to perform and only an hour in which to perform it. One of the members of Monica's Kosciusko Silent No More group really stepped up to the plate and produced two multicolor printed playbills featuring both Mourdock and Lugar for the display cases. It looked like we were advertising for a heavyweight fight rather than a straw poll. In retrospect, we were. He also created nine pole signs, one for each of our nine congressional districts. Each sported the district number and a red, white, and blue motif. In the final minutes before the start of the convention, I noticed a man setting up easels to hold the Bill of Rights and the Declaration of Independence. I was not familiar with this individual, so I introduced myself to him and asked if I could be of assistance. He responded simply by saying that he was Killer. I extended my hand and said, "Olive branch." He accepted, and we have worked well together ever since.

The theater had a three-hundred-person seating capacity, and we had reserved nearly two hundred and fifty seats. Fifty-five Tea Party groups from around Indiana attended, and each had the option to have two voting delegates. Also in attendance were Matt Kibbe and two other FreedomWorks staffers, as well as an Indianapolis inner-city black Baptist minister who would be leading us in the customary tradition of opening Tea Party events with prayer.

As Providence would have it, actor Morgan Freeman had proclaimed the night before our convention that the Tea Party was racist and out to get President Obama. This well-worn, baseless statement could not have been better timed. We thank you, Mr. Freeman, for coming out of irrelevancy, if for only a day, to help us out. The media coverage of our event was less than expected; it was not considered newsworthy based on the assumption the results were a foregone conclusion. The Baptist minister and I had met a year earlier when he and an associate had asked to meet with me. During that meeting, we discussed our shared political and religious beliefs. They both had told me of how they had lost over a third of their congregation from their outspoken criticism of liberalism and the Democratic Party's destructive policies toward the black family. We parted as brothers, and as I was leaving, they asked me if they would be accepted in the Tea Party. My answer to them was conveyed in the form of a broad smile and a warm embrace.

An Indianapolis television station came to our event explicitly to question Tea Party members about Freeman's comments. From the stage, I welcomed the convention attendees and recounted that day a year before in an Indianapolis inner-city church as part of my introduction of the minister. I concluded the introduction with the same question that the minister had asked me: Would he be welcome in the Tea Party? The crowd rose in roaring applause as the minister took the podium. The television station would not be getting the story that they wanted; the Baptist minister set the record straight and sent Mr. Freeman back into irrelevancy.

Patriot Paul, dressed in colonial costume, was up next to lead us in the Pledge of Allegiance with a heavy emphasis on "under God." Monica and I both spoke a few lines about what was at stake that day. I told the crowd of the strength we had when we were united. I said that the seeds of the Tea Party had been sown only two years before and now had sprouted into an international movement. We were now seen as a threat to the establishment, and as such we were mocked, ridiculed, and attacked. I concluded my speech by informing my peers that some politicians were now claiming that there was more than one flavor of tea. Holding the symbol of the Tea Party movement in my hand, I proclaimed that there was only one flavor of tea, the original flavor of tea, and that they should not accept any substitute; that flavor was Gadsden yellow, and I waved my Gadsden flag. The crowd was now in a festive and feisty mood, and we could attend to the business at hand. Pat Miller from WOWO 1190 AM radio was back to finish what he had started eight months earlier. Pat spoke about each of the candidates and the journey that Hoosiers for a Conservative Senate had embarked on ten months before. He mentioned the vetting questions and the lack of a response from Senator Lugar. Each candidate was to be given an opportunity to present his case to us. There were two podiums on the stage. Mr. Lugar's empty podium epitomized his rare presence (until recently) in the state.

Richard Mourdock took to his podium and gave a speech that included the story of five men meeting in the back room of a Boston bar over two hundred years ago to discuss an idea that led to the greatest nation the earth had ever witnessed. He told us that we now found this nation in peril and that liberalism, career politicians, and uncontrolled spending had our nation on the brink of collapse. He promised to go to Washington and challenge the status quo and then to return after two terms and to be subject to the same laws as the rest of us. The delegates were next directed to the sealed ballot box. The ballot had a picture of Lugar on the left; any suggestion that his placement might have been designed as a subliminal message to portray him as a leftist was purely conjuncture. Mourdock appeared on the right side of the ballot. The voters checked the square next to the picture of their candidate and tucked the ballot into the box. Ninety-seven delegates cast their votes, and within minutes, the results would be known. To prevent any allegations of unfair voting, we had asked two retired CPAs to tally and certify the vote. They huddled to count the vote as the crowd awaited the results.

As the vote was being counted, FreedomWorks stepped up to the stage and offered us words of encouragement. Matt Kibbe accepted an award on behalf of the statewide Tea Party movement to be displayed in the offices of FreedomWorks in Washington, DC, to serve as inspiration to others. The award read as follows:

Hoosiers for a Conservative Senate presents the Indiana Tea Party Movement Champion of Liberty Award for outstanding effort and achievement in the pursuit of freedom as originally prescribed in the founding documents of our great nation. The selfless willingness of such a diverse group of individuals to unite and work in a cooperative and coordinated effort should serve as a model and inspiration to all those engaged in the fight of preserving this great American experiment.

Certification of the vote was complete, and the CPAs presented a sealed envelope to Miller. Each of the nine Hoosiers for a Conservative Senate district committee representatives then carried their pole signs up onto the stage and placed them in a row to form the flag of the United States in red, white, and blue to the delight of the audience. Each of the district representatives sat in front of his or her respective sign, and Pat Miller approached us with the results of the vote.

In a vote of ninety-six to one, Richard Mourdock overwhelmingly won the straw poll and the long-anticipated endorsement of Hoosiers for a Conservative Senate. Mourdock then returned to the stage to give his acceptance speech. We had done something nearly impossible: we had united in a singular goal, stayed united against all odds, and were now ready to celebrate our success.

We would soon realize that this day was not the end of the game but merely halftime. Tomorrow we would return to the playing field, but this afternoon was reserved for a celebration of our efforts and a rally for our newly chosen candidate. The nearly two hundred fifty convention participants streamed out of the theater and into the Hancock County Courthouse plaza to a waiting crowd celebrating Hoosiers for a Conservative Senate's endorsement of our candidate. The crowd, sporting red Mourdock shirts and waving American flags, were reveling in patriotic song. A red, three-axle dump truck, compliments of the Tipton County Tea Party, pulled up to the site with air horns blowing and raised its bed. The crowd erupted in laughter at the sight of the truck and the message on its sign: "Dump Lugar." The official fall launch of our universally endorsed candidate's campaign had begun.

CHAPTER 14

Attack of the Oxpeckers

Several days before the convention, Tea Party Express had contacted me and commended us for the unity we had achieved. They would be coming to Indianapolis the week after our convention to add their endorsement to ours. This was a major accomplishment and another of the goals we had set many months before. This was just the beginning of the fruits of our labor. We were hungry for more and waited in anticipation of another endorsement, one that would provide us with the tools to compete effectively with the Lugar campaign. This was the endorsement we had sought from our inception as Hoosiers for a Conservative Senate. The long wait was nearly over, but not soon enough for some.

The day after Hoosiers for a Conservative Senate's endorsement of Richard Mourdock for the US Senate, the National Republican Senatorial Committee asked to follow me on Twitter. Imagine that—the good ol' boys at the NRSC in Washington, DC, were interested in what a farm boy from Indiana had to say. It surely could not have had anything to do with the fact that this particular Tea Party member, along with his thousands of friends, was on safari for a RINO.

Many of our supporters expected an immediate endorsement from FreedomWorks even after having been told that it would not take place on the day of our convention. I told them that the endorsement was forthcoming and would be made when the time was right. This caused frustration for many within the movement, including some Hoosiers for a Conservative Senate committee members, but no one was more upset about it than a certain broomstick rider. The very person who had chided me many months earlier for working so hard to earn the endorsement of FreedomWorks was now demanding that endorsement immediately. The Witch sent out statewide e-mails calling for all Tea Party members to contact FreedomWorks and say they were united in support of Mourdock. She was doing all she could to convince people that her efforts were what had secured the endorsement.

On October 21, 2011, FreedomWorks representatives flew into Indianapolis and, with Hoosiers for a Conservative Senate at their side, made their endorsement of Indiana State Treasurer Richard Mourdock. That same day, presidential candidate Herman Cain was in town for a private luncheon, and the Indianapolis area also played host to the state GOP's fall dinner. Wisconsin Congressman Paul Ryan attended that event, but WISH-TV 8 reported that a small Tea Party gathering at an airport hotel stole the spotlight that day with FreedomWorks' endorsement of Mourdock. The next day, Utah Senator Orrin Hatch sent a request to follow me on Twitter. We were making noise and serving notice that we planned to bag a long-elusive RINO; two thousand miles away, another RINO was getting spooked.

The model we had built was catching the attention of others. Indiana's eighth congressional district, better known as the Bloody Eighth, adopted a scaled-down version of our model in their effort to elect Tea Party favorite Kristi Risk over freshman RINO Congressman Larry Buschon in the May primary. We were pleased to be the inspiration for their efforts and absolutely thrilled when a Tea Party leader in Michigan contacted us and asked questions about how to do what we had done. After many weeks of correspondence, we were asked to travel to DeWitt, Michigan, to speak at the inaugural meeting of Michigan 4 Conservative Senate, a statewide Tea

Party initiative whose only goal was to unite in an effort to defeat Senator Debbie Stabenow in Michigan's 2012 US Senate race.

Monica and I traveled to Michigan on November 17, 2011, and shared our story with a room filled with over fifty Tea Party groups. It was a humbling and rewarding experience to see a meeting remarkably similar to the one we had held in Tipton, Indiana, ten months earlier. Also in attendance at that meeting was a representative from FreedomWorks. The end of the meeting saw over a hundred Tea Party leaders step forward in unity and ink their signatures on a familiar scroll. One week later, that scroll found its way to the Washington, DC, offices of Senator Stabenow and a waiting entourage including FreedomWorks, the DC area Tea Party, and the media.

It was not long before Michigan 4 Conservative Senate realized that they too had their version of our toxic trio. Human nature all but guaranteed that our Michigan counterparts would be subjected to the same pettiness, jealousy, and hatred that we had endured so frequently. Never far beneath the surface lurks a willingness to subvert the good of the many for the benefit of the few. Michigan 4 Conservative Senate was set to host its first senatorial debate between the eight Republican candidates in January 2012. Their efforts were met with a barrage of attacks from a handful of alleged Tea Party members claiming to have the best interests of the movement at heart. Letters were written, e-mails blasted out, and Facebook and web pages created, all explaining how this unity somehow corrupted the political process. Not mentioned in these written attacks were the alliances between many of these supposed Tea Party members and a RINO candidate. Some things never change, and the good people in Michigan were not spared from the same kind of attacks that Hoosiers for a Conservative Senate endured. They, however, had the luxury of knowing that the road ahead of them had already been plowed by their Indiana brethren.

We had become a threat to the symbiotic relationship that exists between career politicians and the various hangers-on that they attract. Our senator was a cottage industry all on his own. Staff members with six-figure incomes, lawyers, lobbyists, political protégés, upstart politicians, and earmark recipients all had a vested interest in keeping the old RINO alive and well. There is no more fitting analogy for this situation than the symbiotic relationship that exists between the oxpecker and the rhinoceros. The rhinoceros tolerates the oxpecker because it is of benefit to the beast. It feeds off ticks, larvae, and other parasites, and in return, the rhinoceros is parasite free. The oxpecker will fend off others to protect its interests when it feels they are being threatened. We would soon be attacked by the human equivalent of oxpeckers as we grew closer to bringing down an old RINO.

In December, we began conducting training sessions on the FreedomWorks phone system. We held the training at several sites around the state, and at each one, a Lugar campaign tracker—or spy, if you will—attended. These spies all operated in the same way: they sat alone, took detailed notes, and left with campaign materials. During these sessions, we also began to distribute the first of thousands of yard signs, door hangers, bumper stickers, and other Mourdock campaign materials. At each of these training sessions there were more than fifty Tea Party activists all eager to learn and help do their part to achieve victory. Included in these training sessions was a crash course on the benefit and use of Twitter. All told, we unleashed nearly a hundred new tweeters onto the scene to get our message out to the masses in cyberspace. It was not long afterward that a new front in the war opened up.

The Twitter wars were initially being waged and won by the Lugar campaign and its surrogates. These oxpeckers consisted of Lugar's congressional staff as well as his campaign staff. Later, their ranks swelled to include former staffers, GOP loyalists, and a down-and-out radio show host in northern Indiana. Once our newly trained Twitter warriors emerged on the scene, our army launched a continual barrage of information about Lugar's voting record to discredit the senator. The war primarily raged under the hashtags #RetireLugar, #INSen, #TCOT, and #RedIN. It was not long before our army outnumbered theirs by a four-to-one margin. All those bad votes were tweeted and retweeted to tens of thousands of people throughout the nation. The exponential proliferation of Twitter networks increased the size of our army until it included Tea Party activists from a dozen other states.

On November 30, 2011, an event occurred that went unnoticed at the time but would later prove an embarrassing blow to the Lugar campaign and invoke the ire of the oxpeckers. A man named Greg Wright filed a complaint with the Indiana Elections Commission challenging Senator Lugar's eligibility to be on the ballot. At issue was the little-known fact that Lugar had sold his Indianapolis residence in 1977 and moved to Virginia but continued to use his old address for voting purposes. Wright, a certified fraud examiner, began to research Lugar's background and provided a great deal of ammunition to use against him.

The reason Lugar had first met us in the Marriott Hotel nearly a year earlier was that he stayed there on the rare occasions when he returned to Indiana. Wright's complaint went unnoticed by the loyal Lugar media and gathered dust until a few bloggers started to promote it. Several weeks later, the Mourdock campaign held a press conference at Lugar's old Indianapolis residence to highlight how out-of-touch the senator was. In early February, additional challenges were made to the Indiana Elections Commission and the Marion County Elections Board. The Indiana Elections Commission is chaired by a Lugar supporter, and in January the regular monthly meeting was not held—we believe so that the commissioner would not have to address the issue. To force him to do so, Hoosiers for a Conservative Senate gathered petitions from all nine of Indiana's congressional districts and hosted a press conference outside Governor Daniels's office and delivered them to the governor, demanding that he order the elections commissioner to hear the case. The governor refused, citing his consultation with the state attorney general—another Lugar supporter—and his conclusion that the senator was allowed by state law to live without any Indiana residence indefinitely. The press conference was broadcast by three Indianapolis television stations and a major radio station. Lugar's residency issue was now out in the public, and both the local and national media were running with the story.

Within days of our press conference, the Indiana Elections Commission issued a statement that they would be hearing the challenge to Lugar's eligibility to be on the ballot along with many other candidate challenges. As expected, the four-member commission ruled unanimously in favor of Senator Lugar, citing the opinions of the current and two former state attorney generals. They, along with Lugar's attorneys, argued that the state constitution was unequivocal: "No person shall be deemed to have lost his residence in the state, by reason of his absence, either on business of this state or of the United States." They also referenced an attorney general's advisory opinion issued after Lugar's first Senate election that stated, "If a person has established residency for voting purposes in an Indiana precinct before his or her service in Congress, that residence remains the Congressperson's residence as long as he or she remains on the business of the state or the United States." What was lost from the spirit of the challenge was that the senator had lied about his address. He had continued for thirty-five years to list his old address on his voter registration form. Indiana's secretary of state had been recently convicted on felony charges for doing essentially the same thing. Lugar was not a resident of Indiana and thus should not only have been ineligible to vote but also held accountable for knowingly falsifying his legal address on voting records.

The oxpeckers had a field day with this ruling and jubilantly celebrated in cyberspace by attacking me with accusations and insults. Apparently there was a Lugar supporter at the hearing tweeting about my presence, and he began using Sal Alinsky tactics to vilify me. I was called a racist, a Nazi, and the founder of the Indiana Aryan Brotherhood and ridiculed for my work as a landscaping business owner. The senator's staff had again been reduced to mocking a private citizen as well as that person's engagement in hard and honest work. This was yet another illustration of the elitist mentality of a career politician. One Lugar staffer smugly said in a tweet directed at me, "You do realize that you have absolutely no future in politics after this is over," to which I replied with a single word: "Promise." Another asked, "What are you going to do after May 8 when you cannot wear those tacky black shirts?" Most disturbing of all the Twitter attacks were those that came from Lugar supporters using fake accounts to pose as women of questionable character. Every time I posted a damning Lugar vote, I found two or three of these imposters following me. My guess is that the Lugar supporters were hoping I might engage in conversation with these imposters and use that against me.

Oxpeckers are a nasty brood when they realize their meal ticket is about to be punched for the last time.

Another of the menacing attack birds was a no-name radio show host of a low-watt station in northern Indiana. He sold his objectivity by accepting advertisements on his program from the Lugar campaign. This individual was a purveyor of smear who claimed to be a champion exposing corrupt politicians and all the while hid a closet full of skeletons. He attacked Monica and me with impunity, mocking my profession and her failed political campaign for the school board. I did not hesitate to respond to his Twitter, blog, and radio attacks by calling him out as someone who had run for office as both a Republican and a Democrat. A Democrat supporting Senator Lugar—what else needed to be said to prove our senator was a liberal? This did not deter our nemesis, and he was determined to pay his debt to the Lugar campaign by posting hit pieces on the Tea Party and Hoosiers for a Conservative Senate. As if providentially, I was sent embarrassing information about this oxpecker, which I forwarded to him in a private message on Twitter. His response was yet another Twitter attack against me, and I had to provide him with four bits of this information before his attacks stopped. I afforded him far more decency and respect than he gave me. The information was not made public and will not be as long as he does not continue the character assassinations of Monica, me, and other Tea Party activists engaged in this battle.

Our friend, Tea Party sympathizer Greg Wright, had also filed a challenge to Lugar's residency with the Marion County Elections Board, which was chaired by two Democrats and one Republican. On March 15, 2012, Wright's attorney argued that lying about his address made Lugar ineligible to vote in Indiana. Lugar's high-priced attorneys argued that the United States and Indiana constitutions allowed for Lugar to use someone else's address as his own. The board was unconvinced and split along party lines, ruling two to one that Lugar could remain on the ballot but that he and his wife could not vote in Indiana. Lugar had suffered an embarrassing defeat, and once again the story dominated the media. The Lugar campaign was demoralized and tried desperately to spin the story as an unholy alliance between the Tea Party and the Democrats. One county GOP chairman went so far as to state publicly that the Tea Party was breathing new life into the state Democratic Party. I promptly chided him by stating that if the GOP did its job of culling the herd of RINOs from its ranks, the Tea Party would be able to spend all its time going after Democrats. Lugar's campaign issued a poll showing the senator up by six points and taunted us with the results. But that same poll showed Lugar's numbers falling fast, and our candidate's numbers were peaking at the right time. The chirping tweets of a once-confident flock of oxpeckers fell eerily silent, but Twitter was abuzz with an emboldened army of Tea Party members. All was quiet for now, but the sky began to fill with dark clouds of angry and desperate oxpeckers preparing for a final assault.

CHAPTER 15

———◆———

The Takedown

Senator Lugar's attorneys appealed the decision of the Marion County Elections Board's ruling against his eligibility to vote. His attorneys had asked the judge not to allow Greg Wright or his attorney to attend this hearing. The media was now engaged in a feeding frenzy as bloggers and radio hosts latched on to Lugar's proliferating problems. Lugar and his wife were ineligible to vote in the state he had left thirty-five years before but continued to represent. The simple solution was to establish a residence, but that action would once again drive the story onto the front page of the media. Lugar and his campaign staff wanted this story to die, but the more they fought, the deeper people dug into his background.

Mr. Wright had also discovered that Lugar's reason for supporting earmarks was not the one he had offered the public. He had been quoted as saying that if Congress did not spend this money, the president would, and that the overall amount of earmark spending was an insignificant drop in the bucket compared to the budget as a whole. Through a researcher friend, we discovered that Lugar's earmark recipients returned the favor by making substantial donations to his campaign. One such benefactor of these generous earmarks was none other than Steven the Snake. One of the Snake's companies had received over six million dollars in military contracts, and in return his company had kicked back nearly twenty-five thousand dollars to the Lugar campaign.

The media reported that Lugar and his staff had been bilking taxpayers during all his hotel stays when he returned to Indiana. Lugar had reported these expenses as official government business, but many of his stays were for fundraising trips. This was obviously illegal and a violation of Senate ethics rules. The matter was reported in the media, and Lugar issued a check for fourteen thousand dollars to the US Treasury as a reimbursement. The payment paled in comparison to the cost to his credibility and campaign. Ironically, one of his illegal hotel charges, totaling $380, was for the night of January 21, 2011. That was the night of his swanky country club fundraiser in Carmel, Indiana, the fundraiser that was hastily arranged to counter the statewide Tea Party unity meeting that Hoosiers for a Conservative Senate was holding the next day. The senator raised over four hundred thousand dollars that night and stiffed the taxpayers with a nearly four-hundred-dollar hotel bill. The Tea Party spent less than three hundred dollars the next day on its event and fourteen months later was on the verge of defeating the most powerful RINO in Washington.

The Lugar campaign was demoralized and resigned to nearly certain defeat. There was no sign of fight left in them; however, their oxpeckers were filled with rage at the prospect of losing their host. The Tea Party was strategizing how best to use its resources as the May primary rapidly approached. I was spending nearly fifty hours a week in get-out-the-vote efforts, including delivering yard signs to Mourdock supporters throughout central Indiana. At night I traveled major roadways, along with dozens of other Tea Party activists, placing yard signs at busy intersections. The Tea Party blanketed the state in Retire Lugar and Mourdock for Senate signs. In all of my thousands of miles of travel around the state, not once did I see a pro-Lugar sign. Lugar's campaign was content with slinging mud at our candidate over the airwaves and through telemarketing phone calls. One Tea Party activist told the story of being called by the Lugar campaign five different times, and each time the caller became argumentative when he was not given the answer he wished to receive.

Many other Tea Party activists took their commitment to the cause to new levels. They funded and erected billboards along US 30 in Warsaw, US 31 in Kokomo, and I-69 in Anderson. These signs were paid for by ordinary citizens who donated five, ten, and twenty dollars toward the signs, which cost nearly a thousand dollars apiece. Other citizens erected Burma Shave–style signs, and still others made their vehicles into rolling billboards in support of Richard Mourdock. Also on the march were several hundred activists who placed door hangers on more than twenty thousand doors throughout the state.

I knew that the Tea Party was winning the race from the ferocity of the attacks being launched at Monica and me. In the waning days of the campaign, the oxpeckers (including a liberal Indianapolis political blogger, our down-and-out radio show host nemesis, and the leader of the fake Tea Party group in Hamilton County) all conspired together to derail our grassroots army by trying to discredit us.

The blogger, Howey Doody, wrote a scathing article titled "Horse Race: Tea Party Cells Rebel against Boyer, Fettig," resurrecting the venom that had been spewed a year earlier by the toxic trio and adding to it the slanderous rants of Chuckie the Puppet, leader of the Tea Party of Hamilton County. Chuckie enjoyed being courted by Lugar's political director and had no qualms about having his strings pulled. He took up the long-extinguished torch of hatred that had once been held by the toxic trio and reignited it in an effort to save Lugar's campaign. Included in the blogger's article were Chuckie's comments that the Tea Party had been hijacked by Monica and me and that we were now feeling a backlash from the movement. He went on to claim that our September convention had been a sham and that the straw poll had been rigged. He claimed that only a handful of groups supported Mourdock and that his group had boycotted our event because of it. Heaping even more RINO dung on the pile, Chuckie stated that we had deceived FreedomWorks by lying about our level of unity. Apparently, this political prostitute was not aware of the fact that the president of FreedomWorks had attended our convention and witnessed the fifty-five unified Tea Party groups voting their approval for our candidate and mission.

Also in the article were comments from Howard County GOP Chairman Craig Dunn, who said:

> Since Fettig was picked up for the national Tea Party council, he has tried to speak for the Tea Parties. People just don't realize that the Tea Party movement is only modestly organized. There is no real structure such as a political party. They are just a bunch of pissed off taxpayers who are sick of the direction the nation is headed. As a result, their natural enemies are incumbents. In Indiana, most of your incumbents are Republicans. Tea Party people could care less about nuclear nonproliferation treaties or intricate international agreements. Their concerns are far more local. You have this organizational vacuum that exists, and Fettig has sensed the vacuum and entered it. He can get by with his assumption of leadership until he is whacked publicly.

I was unaware of having been invited to serve on a national Tea Party council; I wish someone had told me about that. Surely Dunn did not mean the FreedomWorks Tea Party Debt Commission on which I served as a commissioner. He certainly could not be referring to the commission that had gathered testimony from thousands of Americans and formulated their input into a plan that proposed to cut over nine trillion dollars from the federal budget over ten years. Not the commission whose members had met for dozens of hours over many months and then traveled to Washington, DC, at their own expense to present their findings to Congress only to be expelled from the US Senate offices by Harry Reid. That commission spoke for nobody but conveyed the messages of the American people only to be silenced by a hostile and arrogant political system. Dunn had only a vague idea what the Tea Party was about, and he insulted us by stating that we were uninformed about national and international issues. I did not know Dunn personally but was aware of him through a mutual friend. I contacted our friend to express my disappointment that a supposed Mourdock supporter would stoop so low as to attack the character of a person he had never met. My friend contacted Dunn and brokered a telephone meeting with him. Dunn admitted to me that he was friends with Howey Doody and knew him to be a liberal and a Lugar supporter. He went on to say that the story was indeed a hit piece and stated that he had been misquoted in a few instances and misled about the intent of the article. The chairman also noted that Howey Doody's allegiance to Lugar stemmed from a taxpayer-funded trip to Russia with the senator to report on Lugar's work on nuclear nonproliferation. Howey had been made to feel important, perhaps for the first time in his life, and in gratitude he had generously repaid the favor. He had lost all vestiges of objectivity in Russia as he willingly acquired the tactics of *Pravda*, disseminating propaganda for the benefit of his benefactor. Dunn ended our conversation with the admission that he could have chosen his words more carefully and steadfastly asserted his support of Mourdock. I told him that I appreciated his candor and that I would take him at his word and thus would hold no animosity toward him.

The article and subsequent airing of it on the hack radio show host's program was nothing more than the dying gasp of the oxpeckers throwing out one last, desperate attempt to save their host by assassinating the character of two Tea Party leaders who, along with their friends and allies, were on the verge of pulling off one of the biggest political upsets in the history of the United States.

As the final weeks of an eighteen-month campaign began to wind down, our momentum and confidence were skyrocketing. We were peaking at just the right time in the campaign, while the Lugar campaign had been reduced to what the *Weekly Standard* characterized as a "death rattle." The media was writing story after story about our race, and the bandwagon was beginning to grow. It is an interesting study in human nature to witness people and groups trying to be a part of a winning team. The Mourdock campaign received endorsements late in the race from the National Rifle Association, Right to Life, and the Club for Growth. Each of these groups was a powerful ally that could very well be the difference between victory and defeat. Together, these allies, along with FreedomWorks, proved to be a formidable challenge to the establishment's most senior RINO. Club for Growth alone announced that it would be investing over $1.5 million in the race. The NRA holds a 75 percent success record with its endorsements. FreedomWorks provided our grassroots army with tens of thousands of yard signs, door hangers, and bumper stickers to cover the state with Richard Mourdock's name. As I reflected on Hoosiers for a Conservative Senate's long battle, I recalled the words of Mark Twain: "In the beginning of a change the patriot is a scarce man, and brave, and hated and scorned. When his cause succeeds, the timid join him, for then it costs nothing to be a patriot."

In a small midwestern state, over sixty Tea Party groups representing tens of thousands of citizens united to serve notice on the nation that the days of politics as usual had ended. No longer would those who drove this nation to the brink of financial disaster be allowed to imperil the birthright of all Americans—the birthright of the gift of freedom bestowed upon us by our Creator, our founders, and all those that gave the ultimate sacrifice to preserve that gift. The political establishment ignored us when, in defiance, we gathered in the millions to protest a government that had forgotten or refused to honor the oath they took to uphold and defend the Constitution. They mocked us when we organized into thousands of small groups to educate ourselves and our neighbors about the political process. They mercilessly attacked us when we united in a cooperative and coordinated effort to effect positive change. Undeterred, we marched on, and from the heartland rose the largest grassroots activist campaign ever waged in the name of wresting power from an icon of Washington elitism. Along the way, we found others joining our ranks, inspired by success and motivated by passion, pride, and love of country. Regardless of the outcome of any particular battle, America's best days are not behind her but rather ahead as a new breed of constitutional patriots set forth to steady and steer our great nation toward a brighter future. State Senator Delph, in the article meant to destroy our movement, stated, "Whoever is able to harmonize them into one force would be kingmaker." Our movement is not interested in making kings; on the contrary, our forefathers fought and died to unshackle themselves from a tyrannical king. What inspires and motivates us are those words written long ago: "When in the course of human events, it becomes necessary for one people to dissolve the political bands which have connected them with another, and to assume the powers of the earth, the separate and equal station to which the Laws of Nature and of Nature's God entitle them, a decent respect to the opinions of mankind requires that they should declare the causes which impel them to the separation."

The rules of the game have been changed, and a new player is lacing up his boots. The people have awakened. Game on.

www.ingramcontent.com/pod-product-compliance
Lightning Source LLC
Chambersburg PA
CBHW030358290526
45785CB00004B/1807